CONTENTS

Nothing is ever achieved without the support and contribution of many friends and colleagues. Kim McCaffrey, Kelly Leddy, and Aimee Williams provided elegant data analyses to support the conclusions presented in this book. Laura Vercler, Kelley Shrock, and Stefoni Bavin reviewed, edited, and provided advice on various portions of this manuscript. Michele Nafziger provided advice on coordination of care issues related to long-term care. Molly Lebel shared a personal story that inspired a portion of the manuscript. Thank you, all. It has been a genuine honor, privilege, and pleasure to work with you.

About the author

Paul Alexander Clark, MPA, MA, CHE, is the Senior Knowledge Manager for Press Ganey Associates. He directs a team of researchers who conduct quantitative and qualitative research to determine best practices for improving patient, employee, and physician satisfaction in healthcare. His team's research supports more than 110 Press Ganey consultants who actively partner with healthcare organizations to help improve the service they provide to patients, employees, and physicians. Clark earned a Master of Public Administration in Science and Technology Policy from George Mason University in Fairfax, VA, a Master of Arts in Bioethics and Healthcare Policy at the Loyola University in Chicago, and a bachelor's degree from the University of Pittsburgh. He is currently a member of the University of North Carolina's Executive MHA program and a Diplomate in the American College of Healthcare Executives.

About Press Ganey

Press Ganey is the healthcare industry's largest independent vendor of satisfaction measurement and improvement services. It specializes in producing tested and reliable satisfaction surveys, comprehensive management reports, and national comparative databases to monitor and improve customer (patient, resident, physician, and employee) satisfaction in healthcare delivery systems. Founded in 1985 and headquartered in South Bend, IN, Press Ganey serves approximately 6,000 healthcare facilities, including 1,454 hospitals, or more than 30% of the total acute care market.

PRESS GANEY®
The Press Ganey Series

Patient
Satisfaction
and the
Discharge
Process

Evidence-based Best Practices

Paul Alexander Clark, MPA, MA, CHE

hcPro | 20 YEARS Since 1986
THE HEALTHCARE COMPLIANCE COMPANY

Patient Satisfaction and the Discharge Process: Evidence-based Best Practices is published by HCPro, Inc.

HCPro, Inc., provides information resources for the healthcare industry.

Paul Alexander Clark, MPA, MA, CHE, Author
Kelly Alhquist, Developmental Editor
Jackie Diehl Singer, Graphic Artist
Jean St. Pierre, Director of Operations
Patrick Campagnone, Cover Designer
Kathryn Levesque, Group Publisher
John Novack, Group Publisher

Advice given is general. Readers should consult professional counsel for specific legal, ethical, or clinical questions. Arrangements can be made for quantity discounts. For more information, contact:

HCPro, Inc.
200 Hoods Lane
P.O. Box 1168
Marblehead, MA 01945
Telephone: 800/650-6787 or 781/639-1872
Fax: 781/639-2982
E-mail: *customerservice@hcpro.com*

Visit HCPro, Inc., at its World Wide Web sites:

www.hcpro.com and *www.hcmarketplace.com*

Rev. 09/2007
21295

Understanding the discharge process

When we talk about the discharge process, we refer to the tasks, procedures, policies, and people necessary to transition a patient from receiving healthcare managed by the provider to either self-management or the care of another healthcare service provider. When patients leave the hospital for home or transfer to a nursing home or other skilled nursing facility, hospital staff engage in similar work activities to enable the delineation, standardization, and continuous improvement of a process.

No universal standard exists for a discharge process. The steps in the process depend on the unique characteristics of the organization, the services provided, and how those services are already organized and delivered. Traditionally, the physician's discharge order signaled the start of the discharge process. But progressive hospitals envision the discharge process beginning before the patient's admission.

Understanding *your* discharge process

Your improvement journey starts by understanding your discharge process as it currently exists. Understanding the process means being able to answer at least two questions:

- What services are currently being delivered?

- What are the steps involved, who is responsible for them, and how do they happen?

Two management tools, a focused improvement worksheet and a process map, can help you answer these questions. These tools can be applied to any service or process within a service.

Focused improvement worksheet
The focused improvement worksheet (see Figure A.2 in Appendix A) helps you to identify the primary customer needs or wants, the costs involved in satisfying those needs, the locations involved and the connections between them, and tactics for communicating with your customers before, during, and after the service encounter.

The first column, Customer Needs, outlines the ideal customer experience. Information about customer needs can be gathered from your own patient satisfaction surveys, patient comments, focus groups, complaint databases, or other customer listening mechanisms. In addition to what the patient wants, prevailing standards, relevant regulations, and best practices will inform your vision of the ideal as well.

Next, you will honestly document the Current Position—what is being delivered right now. For example, in the Place row, the patient may want his or her prescription brought to the room before discharge (Customer Needs column), but you currently make the patient or family member visit the hospital pharmacy (Current Position column). With this analysis, the gaps between the optimal experience for patient satisfaction and the status quo become readily apparent.

In the final column, Required Steps, you identify the specific changes you want to tackle and the steps required to achieve those changes. This book will provide you with a bevy of knowledge to populate that last column.

Process map

The process map displays in a process flowchart all events, decisions, and steps in the discharge process. Whereas the focused improvement worksheet provides insight into the customer experience of a service process, the process map details the operational nuts and bolts—that is, how the service process actually works. This map helps everyone involved in the process and on your improvement team to visually understand how the process currently works and his or her place in it. Each step in the process provides a potential leverage point to adjust the discharge process for speed, productivity, cost, customer satisfaction, safety, and other outcomes. Figure A.1 in Appendix A shows a sample portion of a discharge process map.[1] Many consider it important to create a flowchart of any new proposed process to determine whether you implemented every intervention identified in the focused improvement worksheet.

Understanding what the patient wants

Stated simply:

> . . . patients want to be taken seriously both as patients and as real people whose family and social and economic lives have been threatened or disrupted by the medical problem and by the isolation and disorientation of hospitalization.[2]

Although this topic will be more thoroughly treated in Chapter 1, momentarily consider the patient's perspective. Truly suffering from the illness experience, patients and families need every interaction to support, affirm, and help them on their road to recovery or to help ameliorate their physical, mental, and emotional pain when recovery is not possible. Evaluate and design every process with these goals in mind. Specifically, within the discharge process, patients want to

- know when they will be going home and what they have to go through on the day of discharge.

- feel safe. They want to feel like they're ready and prepared to go home or to transition elsewhere.

- have the information they need to feel truly prepared not simply to go home but also to care for themselves in the days after discharge.

- experience a convenient, easy, fast, and pain-free transition from their hospital bed to home.

- have their follow-up care and home care seamlessly arranged.

- actually go home.

- have all their questions answered, their feelings considered, their family involved, flexibility in the process to adjust to their needs, and a continuous healing relationship with their care providers.

All of these points require effective communication from nurses, doctors, and anyone else who interacts with patients or family members.

Recent studies have substantially increased the body of knowledge and understanding of patients' informational and educational needs in preparation for discharge.[3] Patients want information about follow-up, home care, symptom management, pain management, and coping with potential health problems.[4] They want specific written information and resources on follow-up and community services,[5] pain treatment,[6] and life activities (e.g., what the patient can and cannot do).[7] In fact, Gustafson et al.[8] found that information and support needs of patients outweighed care delivery needs and service concerns. Despite the value of and demand for this general information, however, between 27% and 80% of patients do not receive the amount of information they want.[9]

Clinically related educational needs are also slipping through the cracks. Rowe et al.[10] surveyed patients following a stay of five days or less and found that more than 50% failed to receive information about side effects, recovery at home, or community health services. Jones et al.[11] found that 81% of patients needing assistance with basic functional needs failed to receive home care referrals, and 64% of those patients reported that no one at the hospital had talked to them about managing care at home. A post-discharge follow-up study found that 50% of patients who depended on others for basic functional needs did not receive home care referrals.[12] And in a recent study by Bowles et al.,[13] more than 56% of patients discharged did not receive a home care referral despite being screened into the study on the basis of this need and being at risk for poor discharge outcomes; 96% of these patients had unmet discharge needs. Such studies confirm observations that, as a side effect of U.S. healthcare consumerism, patients and families have assumed greater direct responsibility for their own care, and that care is often complex and dangerous.[14]

Patients' postdischarge care needs, usually undertaken by their families, range from errands, household chores, and basic functional needs (e.g., bathing, getting dressed), to nontrivial medical needs (e.g., changing dressings, wound care, help with physical therapy regimens).[15] The majority of caregivers care for patients' personal needs following hospitalization, and 75% assume responsibility for five or more tasks (e.g., preparing meals, administering medication, etc.).[16] However, caregivers often do not feel adequately prepared to assume these responsibilities.[17] Increasingly, we see that caregiving takes an emotional and physical toll on patients' families, resulting in higher rates of depression, injury, and physical illness among those family members with caregiving responsibilities. Clearly, the illness of one patient affects a whole family. That family-oriented approach is an emergent patient need in the discharge process.

What patients typically receive

Another part of the problem is that patients and families who do receive hospital discharge planning, counseling, home care referrals, and other social interventions often do not find these interventions beneficial, indicating that the way in which many hospitals currently conduct the discharge process is not effective in meeting needs.[18] In other words, the status quo is not good enough. Posthospital needs for care, assistance, and information (e.g., activity limitations) remain[19]; discharge plans often are not implemented as planned[20]; and home care services deviate from discharge plans or unexpectedly terminate within a few weeks after discharge.[21] Nurses routinely underestimate patients' needs at discharge, overestimate the quality and amount of education and information provided, and fail to discern the needs that

 Patient Satisfaction and the Discharge Process

patients and caregivers find important.[22] Yet those of us working in hospitals typically don't know this, because it arises *after* discharge, so we don't see or hear of it. Only through patient feedback are we able to know about those first critical days postdischarge.

The discharge process is likely the final impression that the hospital and staff will leave on the memories of patients and their families. A good experience leaves the patient with positive emotions and a strong affinity for returning to the facility. A negative experience can override the good impressions and positive considerations that were formed throughout the patient's stay in the hospital. This is the moment of truth, when patients see whether they are actually cared for as a person or whether they are just another bed occupant who needs to be "streeted" as quickly as possible. It's clear that for the majority of the hospitals, the latter happens more frequently than we would want.

The prevailing standards

Among other things, practitioners are also guided by the American Medical Association (AMA) and the Joint Commission on Accreditation of Healthcare Organizations (JCAHO), which provide comprehensive standards for a quality discharge process, patient education, and continuity of care (see Table A.1 in Appendix A).

JCAHO requires patient education based on robust requirements, including an in-depth learning needs assessment; detailed education about medication, nutrition, hygiene, and techniques to help patients function independently; contact information for community resources and where to obtain further treatment; and discharge instructions for patients, families, and caregivers. JCAHO requires the education to be interactive, planned, supported, and coordinated by the hospital in an interdisciplinary and collaborative fashion, with all resources provided to the patient and family at no cost. The "goal of patient and family education is to improve patient health outcomes by promoting healthy behavior and involving the patient in care and care decisions."[23] However, significant evidence calls into question whether these standards are actually being delivered in most U.S. hospitals; odds are good that, for most hospitals, these standards represent goals.[24]

Why the discharge process is important

The discharge process is

- fundamental to patients' satisfaction and loyalty; it affects the direct, long-term financial return-on-investment through loyal patients.[25]

- significantly linked to the patient care experience, which is most strongly predictive of physician satisfaction and loyalty; patients and physicians converge most strongly in their agreement that the discharge process represents a strong opportunity for improvement in most hospitals because, like patients, physicians want a fast, efficient, and effective discharge process.

- critical to patient flow—your organization's ability to move patients through the care processes efficiently and produce a good return on assets.

- imperative to patient safety and clinical quality. The discharge process involves educating patients on medication usage, therapy regimens, self-care in light of illness, and basic self-care knowledge (of which many people have little awareness or misinformation). Actually changing behavior to achieve patient adherence demands more than passively sending information along.

- a component in nearly every national and regional public reporting initiative for hospital quality. The Centers for Medicare & Medicaid Services' (CMS) Hospital Care Quality Information from the Consumer Perspective (HCAHPS) initiative, HospitalCompare.gov, the California Hospital Assessment and Reporting Taskforce, U.S. News & World Report, and many other regional publicly reported quality comparisons continue to burgeon as the market demands transparency.

This last factor deserves special consideration because it ties together issues that typically receive board priority. First, publicly reported quality measures affect patient and physician hospital **selection decisions**. Patients' perception of and satisfaction with the hospital experience will be the measure most frequently used by consumers—more than clinical quality measures—because the concept of customer satisfaction is easiest to understand.

Second, the institution's **reputation** within its market is at stake. These measures are widely reported by

Patient Satisfaction and the Discharge Process

news organizations, consumer-oriented data aggregators (such as HealthGrades), and insurers' patient decision-making aids (such as Subimo). Further, the data are, of course, as available to the competition as to the public.

Finally, this data will eventually affect **reimbursement** if, as many consider inevitable, the CMS diagnosis-related group payment system is realigned to incentivize quality and pay for performance. With the strong prospect of incentives tied to HCAHPS participation, administrators will take renewed, vigorous interest in the measurement and improvement of patients' perceptions.[26] HCAHPS has a specific section devoted to "When you left the hospital." Even if direct reimbursement does not emerge, the best practices discussed in this book hold inherent benefits in financial returns via improved quality, satisfaction, and loyalty. Doing what it takes to improve your patients' satisfaction with the discharge process will also improve your process efficiency, patient flow, and medical staff satisfaction—all of which have financial implications for return on investment (ROI).

Chapter 1 will introduce and analyze dasta from the patient's perspective on discharge, project the implications of HCAHPS, and consider synergistic ROI benefits. For each of the four components of the discharge process, Chapters 2–5 will analyze the causes of patient satisfaction and dissatisfaction and present evidence-based best practices to address these causes. Chapter 6 will express further best practices for focused improvement. Finally, Chapter 7 will summarize what it takes to create and maintain a strong, well-mechanized discharge process at your facility.

References

1. D. Anthony and others, "Re-engineering the Hospital Discharge: An Example of a Multifaceted Process Evaluation," *Advances in Patient Safety* 2 (2005): *www.ahrq.gov/downloads/pub/advances/vol2/Anthony.pdf.*

2. I. Press. *Patient Satisfaction: Understanding and Managing the Experience of Care*, 2nd ed. (Chicago: ACHE Press), 2006.

3. N. Bubela and others, "Factors influencing patients' informational needs at time of hospital discharge," *Patient Education and Counseling* 16 (1990): 21–28; J. Bostrom and others, "Learning needs of hospitalized and recently discharged patients." *Patient Education and Counseling* 23 (1994): 83–89; S. K. Armitage and K. M. Kavanagh, "Consumer-orientated outcomes in discharge planning: A pilot

study," *Journal of Clinical Nursing* 7, no. 1 (1998): 67–74; M. Lithner and T. Zilling, "Pre- and post-operative information needs," *Patient Education and Counseling* 40 (2000): 29–37; M. Burney, M. Purden, and L. McVey, "Patient satisfaction and nurses' perceptions of quality in an inpatient cardiology population," *Journal of Nursing Care Quality* 16 (2002): 56–67; D. H. Gustafson and others, "Increasing understanding of patient needs during and after hospitalization," *Joint Commiss-ion Journal on Quality Improvement* 27 (2001): 81–92; E. W. Jones, P. M. Densen, and S. D. Brown, "Posthospital needs of elderly people at home: Findings from an eight-month follow-up study." *Health Services Research* 24 (1989): 643–664; P. Reiley and others, "Learning from patients: A discharge plan-ning improvement project," *Joint Commission Journal on Quality Improvement* 22, no. 5 (1996): 311–322.

4. S. K. Armitage and K. M. Kavanagh, "Consumer-orientated outcomes in discharge planning: A pilot study," *Journal of Clinical Nursing* 7, no. 1 (1998): 67–74; M. Lithner and T. Zilling, "Pre- and post-operative information needs," *Patient Education and Counseling* 40 (2000): 29–37; M. Burney, M. Purden, and L. McVey, "Patient satisfaction and nurses' perceptions of quality in an inpatient cardiology population," *Journal of Nursing Care Quality* 16 (2002): 56–67.

5. M. Lithner and T. Zilling, "Pre- and postoperative information needs," *Patient Education and Counseling* 40 (2000): 29–37; P. Reiley and others, "Learning from patients: A discharge planning improvement project," *Joint Commission Journal on Quality Improvement* 22, no. 5 (1996): 311–322.

6. M. Lithner and T. Zilling, "Pre- and postoperative information needs," *Patient Education and Counseling* 40 (2000): 29–37; M. Burney, M. Purden, and L. McVey, "Patient satisfaction and nurses' perceptions of quality in an inpatient cardiology population," *Journal of Nursing Care Quality* 16 (2002): 56–67.

7. M. Lithner and T. Zilling, "Pre- and postoperative information needs," *Patient Education and Counseling* 40 (2000): 29–37.

8. D. H. Gustafson and others, "Increasing understanding of patient needs during and after hospitaliza-tion," *Joint Commission Journal on Quality Improvement* 27 (2001): 81–92.

9. M. Burney, M. Purden, and L. McVey, "Patient satisfaction and nurses' perceptions of quality in an

 Patient Satisfaction and the Discharge Process

inpatient cardiology population," *Journal of Nursing Care Quality* 16 (2002): 56–67; K. R. Jones, R. E. Burney, and B. Christy, "Patient expectations for surgery: Are they being met?" *Joint Commission Journal on Quality Improvement* 26 (2000): 349–360.

10. W. S. Rowe and others, "Variables impacting on patients' perceptions of discharge from short-stay hospitalisation or same-day surgery," *Health and Social Care in the Community* 8 (2000): 362–371.

11. E. W. Jones, P. M. Densen, and S. D. Brown, "Posthospital needs of elderly people at home: Findings from an eight-month follow-up study." *Health Services Research* 24 (1989): 643–664.

12. M. A. Rosswurm and D. M. Lanham, "Discharge planning for elderly patients," *Journal of Gerontological Nursing* 24 (1998): 14–21.
13. K. H. Bowles, M. D. Naylor, and J. B. Foust, "Patient characteristics at hospital discharge and a comparison of home care referral decisions," *Journal of the American Geriatric Society* 50, no. 2 (2002): 336–342.

14. I. Morrison, *Health Care in the New Millennium: Vision, Values, and Leadership* (San Francisco: Jossey-Bass), 2000.

15. I. Wolock and others, "The posthospital needs and care of patients: Implications for discharge planning," *Social Work in Health Care* 12 (1987): 61–76.

16. C. DesRoches and others, "Caregiving in the post-hospitalization period: Findings from a national survey," *Nursing Economics* 20 (2002): 216–221, 224.

17. J. S. Leske and S. A. Pelczynski, "Caregiver satisfaction with preparation for discharge in a decreased-length-of-stay cardiac surgery program," *Journal of Cardiovascular Nursing* 14 (1999): 35–43.

18. M. F. Jackson, "Discharge planning: Issues and challenges for gerontological nursing. A critique of the literature," *Journal of Advanced Nursing* 19, no. 3 (1994): 492–502; K. A. vom Eigen and others, "Carepartner experiences with hospital care," *Medical Care* 37, no. 1 (1999): 33–38.

19. J. S. Oktay and others, "Evaluating social work discharge planning services for elderly people:

Access, complexity, and outcome," *Health and Social Work* 17, no. 4 (1992): 290–298; J. Mamon and others, "Impact of hospital discharge planning on meeting patient needs after returning home," *Health Services Research* 27, no. 2 (1992): 155–175.

20. E. K. Proctor, N. Morrow-Howell, and S. J. Kaplan, "Implementation of discharge plans for chronically ill elders discharged home," *Health and Social Work* 21, no. 1 (1996): 30–40.

21. E. P. Simon and others, "Delivery of home care services after discharge: What really happens," *Health and Social Work* 20, no. 1 (1995): 5–14.

22. J. H. Rose, K. F. Bowman, and D. Kresevic, "Nurse versus family caregiver perspectives on hospitalized older patients: An exploratory study of agreement at admission and discharge," *Health Communication* 12, no. 1 (2000): 63–80.

23. L. D. Phillips. Patient education: Understanding the process to maximize time and outcomes. *Journal of Intravenous Nursing* 22, no. 1 (1999): 19–35.

24. P. A. Clark and others, "Patient perceptions of quality in discharge instruction," *Patient Education and Counseling* 59, no. 1 (2005): 56–68.

25. E. C. Nelson and others, "Do patient perceptions of quality relate to hospital financial performance?" *Journal of Health Care Marketing* 12 (1992): 6–13.

26. J. Conn, "Mandating H-CAHPS?" *Modern Healthcare* (January 16, 2006).

What the data says: Going home from the patient's perspective

Going home is perhaps the most welcomed, appreciated, and greatly anticipated event in a hospital stay. Take a moment, close your eyes, and think about **your home.** Think about your loved ones, your comfortable bed, your pets, and your home-cooked food. Consider the familiar surroundings that make you feel relaxed, comfortable, and happy. Home is the place that grounds you. It is a place where you don't have an unfamiliar roommate, hall noise, 3:00 a.m. blood draws, or metal bars along the sides of your bed. After considering this, you can understand why patients' desire to go home is so strong. We all would rather be home than in a medical facility.

Nevertheless, going home doesn't happen instantly after the pain subsides. Getting patients to the point where they can physically manage on their own, arranging ongoing care, and helping patients and family understand what they need to do are all part of going home. This is typically a complex, interdisciplinary, multi-organization process.

Patients evaluate this process based on four distinct elements. Press Ganey identified these elements through ethnographic and qualitative research by developing survey instruments to measure patients' satisfaction with their experience of care and then testing these elements against rigorous psychometric standards.[1] Broadly conceived, these four elements are as follows:

1. **Patient's personal readiness.** Do the patient and family feel that they have the appropriate understanding, confidence, and capacity to manage at home? Patients with serious concerns about their own ability to manage typically will have real issues that need to be addressed.

2. **Speed.** Is the process of getting the patient home efficient?

3. **Instruction.** Do patients and family members know what to do after they are discharged? Was patient education regarding self-care, therapy, medication, and other issues effective?

4. **Coordination of arrangements across the continuum.** With our aging population, more patients now require home care services, medical equipment, rehabilitation care, and other health services postdischarge. How well were these arrangements made and communicated?

Four specific points that comprise the discharge section of Press Ganey's Inpatient Satisfaction Surveys explicitly measure these broad concepts:

1. Extent to which you felt ready to be discharged
2. Speed of discharge process after you were told you could go home
3. Instructions given about how to care for yourself at home
4. Help with arranging home care services (if needed)

A correlation analysis demonstrates that each of these items factors into patients' overall satisfaction with their care and future loyalty behaviors, particularly "likelihood to recommend," which is a powerful measure of future behavioral intention, and "word-of-mouth" effects (see Table 1.1). Thus, when patients think back on and judge their experiences at your facility, one of the things they will consider is their experience with the discharge process. *How* they evaluate their discharge experience is determined by the four factors above. If you wish to create a patient-centered discharge process, build your changes on these critical leverage points.

TABLE **Correlation analysis of the discharge section**

Correlation analysis of the discharge section of the survey with overall satisfaction and patient loyalty as measured by "Likelihood to recommend . . . "

Based on responses received in 2004 from 2,178,609 patients treated at 1,506 facilities.	Likelihood of your recommending hospital	Overall rating of care given at hospital
Extent to which felt ready to be discharged	0.434	0.422
Speed of discharge process	0.455	0.442
Instructions about how to care for self at home	0.519	0.545
Help with arranging home care services	0.524	0.541

More than 1,500 hospitals nationwide currently incorporate these questions into their continuous quality measurement and improvement processes. From working with our partners on these issues, we see that patient satisfaction scores for these questions fluctuate as a direct result of improvement interventions, staffing levels, and other management and quality changes. They are true indicators of service quality delivered by everyone involved in the discharge process, including the internal service quality from support functions. Conversely, we also see instances of scores not changing when nothing is done to actually change the patient's reality in the discharge process. One of our favorite proverbs is "You can't fatten the cow by weighing it." That is, management discussion alone—no matter how heated—does not change daily practice on the front lines. Measurement alone does nothing; one must take action. Therefore, use your facility's quantitative and qualitative patient data to make changes in the services and process. The stories and practices we relate here are all examples of some person—typically a mid-level manager or director—taking action with his or her patient satisfaction data to change the reality of the patient's journey home.

Note that, according to an analysis of the Press Ganey National Inpatient Database, patients perceive the discharge process as a discrete series of events, exclusive of the main hospital experience. Thus, the four questions within the discharge section are highly interdependent—improving one aspect of the discharge process is highly likely to improve the other discharge items as well. Using multiple interventions simultaneously will enhance the efficacy of many best practices.

Implications for national public reporting

In 2006, the Centers for Medicare & Medicaid Services (CMS) will launch the national patient perspectives public reporting initiative, Hospital CAHPS: Patient Perspectives on Care (HCAHPS). Participating hospitals will have their patients' evaluations publicly available at the CMS Hospital Compare Web site (*www.hospitalcompare.hhs.gov*). Like the Press Ganey survey, HCAHPS contains a section devoted to the discharge process (see Table 1.2) and focuses on managing at home, instruction, and coordination of care.

We conducted an analysis of the data from HCAHPS trial runs and compared hospitals' performance in the Press Ganey discharge section to the HCAHPS discharge section. Press Ganey's discharge section was a strong, reliable predictor of performance in the HCAHPS discharge section. Given the looming prospects of public reporting, many hospitals consider it strategically important

to measure and improve not just HCAHPS measures but their predictors or precursors on the Press Ganey survey as well.

1.2 TABLE

HCAHPS discharge process questions

When you left the hospital

18. After you left the hospital, did you go directly to your own home, to someone else's home, or to another health facility?
   1 ☐ Own home
   2 ☐ Someone else's home
   3 ☐ Another health facility

If Another, Go to Question 21

19. During this hospital stay, did doctors, nurses or other hospital staff talk with you about whether you would have the help you needed when you left the hospital?
   1 ☐ Yes
   2 ☐ No

20. During this hospital stay, did you get information in writing about what symptoms or health problems to look out for after you left the hospital?
   1 ☐ Yes
   2 ☐ No

Synergy: Patients, physicians, and hospitals win-win-win

Information provided during discharge helps patients feel more confident in the management of their health.[2] Standard communication, such as "Is there anything you need or want to know?" on the morning of discharge will ensure that the hospital addresses any lingering information needs.[3] Education and information can then be provided and tailored to the patients' and families' expressed needs.

Despite this, patients' feelings of confidence may not last—they may feel well informed at the point of discharge, but this perception may deteriorate over time. Henderson and Zernike found that within one or two weeks after discharge, patients felt substantially less well informed.[4]

This finding underscores the importance of surveying patients soon after discharge (within the first 10 days) as well as the need for follow-up interventions that we will detail in Chapter 5.

Once home, a patient can use written instructions as a continuous information resource (e.g., they could outline what to do at home, when to resume life activities, symptoms to look out for, and the contact information of someone on the healthcare team). Patients want clear, understandable instructions.[5] In addition, postdischarge telephone follow-up can help address ongoing information needs. Several studies have shown significant increases in patient satisfaction and improved clinical outcomes when members of the healthcare team phone patients within two weeks following discharge.[6] Patients clearly win when their experience translates into better physical outcomes.

One research finding that amazes healthcare professionals is this: Patients who experience longer stays at hospitals are significantly less satisfied—no matter what their diagnosis. The data tells us that, typically, patients want to go home at least as much as the hospital staff want to see them go home. Most salient is the prospect that, by reducing length of stay, facilities can simultaneously achieve higher patient satisfaction and significant cost savings.

Another important convergence that Press Ganey's research has recently discovered is in the arena of *physician satisfaction*. When analyzing the patient's evaluation of the hospital and comparing it to the physician's evaluation of the same hospital, we find that one of the strongest predictors of physician satisfaction with the quality of patient care and the patients' perspective is *discharge*. Despite the vast sociocultural differences between the typical physician and patient, both agree that an effective discharge process is important to their overall evaluation of quality of care.

Finally, because organizational support for service and quality improvement projects result, in large part, from senior executives' perception of the program's payoffs, let's review the financial benefits of patient satisfaction.[7] As a dimension of hospital quality,

> *Discharge is significantly related to earnings per bed (p < 0.003). For earnings per bed, the dollar amount associated with a one point gain or loss in satisfaction (e.g., moving from an average rating of "good" = 3 points to "very good" = 4 points) for this dimension of quality is $4980.[8]*

These facts and the powerful bond between overall patient satisfaction and patient loyalty, likelihood to recommend, and measures of financial performance[9] should provide ample justification for dedicating resources to improving the quality of discharge preparation.

How to use the next four chapters

The following four chapters of this book center on the four areas of discharge planning: readiness, speed, self-care, and follow-up. Each chapter starts with a fishbone diagram that expresses the different events, both with the patient and the hospital, that can cause an unpleasant discharge experience. And because any unpleasant experience may lead to lower patient satisfaction scores, best practices are provided to counter these negative events. These best practices are real protocols used by hospitals across the nation in an effort to raise satisfaction scores.

Each best practice is also ordered by rank and level of evidence. The bolded best practices are those that have been validated by original qualitative research conducted by Press Ganey. A majority of the best-performing or most-improved hospitals utilized these particular practices in improving or maintaining performance. The levels are broken down in Table 1.3.

    Patient Satisfaction and the Discharge Process

1.3 Levels of evidence for best practices

- **Level I:** Systematic literature review of randomized controlled trials (RCT). The practice has proven by multiple RCTs to improve patient satisfaction. Review searches for the existence of any evidence to the contrary and factors such evidence into consideration.

- **Level II:** RCTs in which at least one study has shown a cause and effect. Limitations usually apply, as RCTs frequently draw on limited populations.

- **Level III::** Pseudo-randomized, comparative studies with control and comparative studies with historical control. Limitations always apply to the generalizability of these studies.

- **Level IV:** Case series or case study. Usually uncontrolled; therefore, cause and effect cannot be assumed. Practice used, possibly as part of a cadre of interventions. Holds only the potential for efficacy. Serious limitations on generalizability.

- **Level V:** Unpublished studies of interventions to improve patient satisfaction. Usually not controlled. Almost always one component of several interventions or an overarching organizational change. Cause and effect cannot be determined.

Read a full explanation of how Press Ganey categorizes its best practices in Appendix B.

When resources and finances are limited, it's important to focus on improvements that will offer the best advantage of your facility. These levels will help you to make a more informed decision about which practices your facility might choose to pursue.

References

1. D. O. Kaldenberg and others, "Patient-derived information: Satisfaction with care and post-acute care environments" in *Measuring and managing health care quality: Procedures, techniques, and protocols*, 2nd ed., eds. N. Goldfield, M. Pine, and J. Pine (New York: Aspen Publishers), 2002, 4:69–4:89.

2. A. Henderson and W. Zernike, "A study of the impact of discharge information for surgical patients," *Journal of Advanced Nursing* 35 (2001): 435–441.

3. A. J. Tierney and others, Meeting patients' information needs before and after discharge from hospital," *Journal of Clinical Nursing* 9 (2000): 859–860.

4. A. Henderson and W. Zernike, "A study of the impact of discharge information for surgical patients," *Journal of Advanced Nursing* 35 (2001): 435–441.

5. A. Robinson and M. Miller, "Making information accessible: Developing plain English discharge instructions," *Journal of Advanced Nursing* 24, no. 3 (1996): 528–535.

6. V. Dudas and others, "The impact of followup telephone calls to patients after hospitalization," *American Journal of Medicine* 111 (2001): 26S–30S; J. R. Nelson, "The importance of post-discharge telephone follow-up for hospitalists: A view from the trenches," *American Journal of Medicine* 111 (2001): 43S–44S; W. R. Gombeski Jr. and others, "Patient callback program: A quality improvement, customer service, and marketing tool," *Journal of Health Care Marketing* 13 (1993): 60–65; T. Laughlin and P. Colwell, "Leaving the hospital: Satisfaction with the discharge process," The *Satisfaction Monitor* [newsletter], March/April 2002, *www.pressganey.com/research/resources/satmon/text/bin/135.shtm*; J. Bostrom and others, "Telephone follow-up after discharge from the hospital: Does it make a difference?" *Applied Nursing Research* 9 (1996): 47–52.

7. B. K. Redman and others, "Organizational resources in support of patient education programs: relationship to reported delivery of instruction," *Patient Education and Counseling* 9 (1987): 177–197.

8. E. C. Nelson and others, "Do patient perceptions of quality relate to hospital financial performance?" *Journal of Health Care Marketing* 12 (1992): 6–13.

9. J. W. Peltier and others, "By now it's accepted: patient loyalty that lasts a lifetime experiences with hospital staff can make or break relationships," *Marketing Health Services* 22 (2002): 29; J. John, "Referent opinion and health care satisfaction: Patients' evaluations of hospital care can be linked to how they select the provider," *Journal of Health Care Marking* 14 (1994): 24; J. E. Ware Jr. and A. R. Davies, "Behavioral consequences of consumer dissatisfaction with medical care," *Evaluation and Program Planning* 6 (1983): 291–297; M. Drain and D. C. Kaldenberg, "Building patient loyalty and trust: The role of patient satisfaction," *Group Practice Journal* October (1998); I. Press and others, "Satisfied patients can spell financial well-being," *Healthcare Financial Management* 45 (1991): 34–36; R. Bell and M. J. Krivich, *How to use patient satisfaction data to improve healthcare quality*, (Milwaukee, WI: ASQ Quality Press, 2000).

Extent to which you felt ready to be discharged

Learning objectives

By the end of this chapter, you should be able to

- consider what hospitals might do to make patients feel rushed

- identify potential hospital and patient causes for patient dissatisfaction with readiness for discharge

- review best practices designed to address these root causes

- discuss why it is important to have varied educational resourses

Cause and effect fishbone diagram for patient's readiness for discharge

2.1 FIGURE

PATIENT CAUSES

Patient feels rushed

1. Patient still feels sick/in pain

2. Patient doesn't fully understand his or her illness

3. Patient doesn't feel capable of self care

4. Patient has not seen a physician recently

5. Patient expected or feels illness warrants a longer stay

Patient experiences uncertainty, distress, or difficulties

6. Patient fears something will go wrong now that he or she is away from expert care

Experiences unmemorable, at best; at worst, dissatisfying

7. Patient/caregiver experiences emotional distress the day of discharge

8. Patient feels lack of control in the process; needs remain unmet

Effect

Low score for "Extent to which you felt ready to be discharged"

1. Bed shortage rushes the discharge process

2. Physicians, nurses, and specialists provided conflicting information about when patient could go home

3. There is no opportunity for gradual recovery and extended consideration of postdischarge options

4. Standard discharge procedures not patient-centered

5. No customer service procedure in place to impress patients as they leave

HOSPITAL CAUSES

2.2 FIGURE

Summary of best practices

Level I	• **Comprehensive discharge planning for as many patients as possible**
Level II	
Level III	
Level IV	• **Patient question sheet** • Preadmission patient education • **Service protocols to elicit and address needs, existing and anticipated** • Ongoing assessments and fulfillment of patients' educational needs • Confirm that the patient has acquired the skills/services necessary to manage at home • Physician provides closure • **Protocols to manage the patient's expectations regarding length of stay** • Contact information sheet • **Customer service or behavioral standards** • Techniques for enhancing the patient's perception of involvement • Improving overall patient flow • White board with expected discharge date • Step-down unit • **Make leaving the hospital a memorable event**
Level V	• Examine day of discharge processes for possible redesign

Best practices in bold are those validated by original qualitative reseach conducted by Press Ganey For information on the levels, see Table 1.3.

For patients, discharge from the hospital is a serious and complex transition. It may be just the beginning of coping with the full, blunt, and sometimes frightening force of their medical condition—without the comprehensive support of nurses and physicians. Their stay in your facility will not have been a success unless they are prepared with the knowledge, skills, understanding, and confidence they need to care for themselves. In addition, as the length of time that patients stay in hospitals decreases, discharge planning and transitional nursing care become more important. Patients often need to continue a treatment regimen or recovery plan after they leave, and staff must educate patients and provide them with sufficient training in preparation for their discharge. They may need to counsel patients or convince them that they are capable of managing at home—either on their own or with the help of family or home care services. In addition, when patients are discharged, staff must affirm that they are ready to go home, even when it would be comforting to the patient to stay longer.

The fishbone diagram at the beginning of this chapter details several potential sources of dissatisfaction, some caused by the patient and some caused by the hospital. Although this list is not exhaustive, it is a good starting place for exploring the issues at your facility. Conducting a root-cause analysis session with your staff and completing a fishbone diagram is a useful exercise, not only to identify issues, but also to engage staff in thinking about the customer's experience and perception of events that have become daily routine for associates. Let's explore possible causes of patient dissatisfaction with discharge readiness.

Patient causes

1. The patient still feels sick/in pain

Patients often enter the hospital seeking to be cured. They expect their illness to be resolved or a specific procedure to be performed that will cure them. They may not anticipate a significant period of home recuperation or know how they will actually feel.

Best practice: Patient question sheet (Level IV)

Encourage patients to write questions for physicians or nurses throughout the hospitalization experience. Provide a sheet explicitly for this purpose. Begin at admission or preadmission with prompts designed to manage expectations and elicit patients' thinking. Nurses and physicians should be aware of and trained to check this sheet (which should be included in the medical charts). At the point of discharge, review the sheet with the patient and ensure that all questions have been answered.

Making it work

Patient white boards

In all patient rooms at Centra Health in Lynchburg, VA, there is a white message board above the patient's bed. This board lists the patient's name, nurses' names, and schedule for the day. It also has a space for family/patient questions and the expected day of discharge.

Note pads

Every patient room in Thomas Hospital in Fairhope, AL, contains a note pad explicitly for the purpose of writing questions as they occur to the patient or family. The note pads display the hospital logo and the phrase "Questions I have." A pen accompanies the pad.

 Patient Satisfaction and the Discharge Process

Best practice: Preadmission patient education (Level IV)

Preadmission patient education is used for common elective procedures (e.g., joint replacement) and covers the surgery, postoperative recovery, and rehabilitation. During this session, explicitly establish

- what symptoms to expect

- what level of pain to expect

- how the patient will feel postop (e.g., "you may feel cold"; "the surroundings may initially be confusing"; etc.)

- what functions may be limited, even initially (e.g., "you won't be allowed to eat for the first few hours after surgery"; "you won't be able to walk for the first day"; etc.)

- what staff will do to relieve these symptoms

Make sure to include information about posthospitalization recovery (e.g., "you may experience some swelling and redness; this is normal"). Make these sessions interactive, and use printed information to improve the likelihood of learning/future recall.

Another preadmission education tool is to let patients and their families tour the unit where they will be staying. While they are present, put them in touch with any support groups that may exist or have them sit in on a group meeting.

Other samples of preoperative education are as follows:

- Interactive sessions with the case manager, patient education nurse, or surgeon using standardized written information that details everything that will happen.

- Videotaped tours of the unit. These videos can outline the procedure, recovery, rehab, etc., and can be sent to the patient.

- Brochures for every surgical procedure that outline the steps involved and what everything will feel like from admission through recovery. Provide the phone numbers for education on medical topics for nurses to reference should the patient have any questions. Send this information to the patient the week before surgery.

- Calls to the patient the day before admission, during which staff ask patients whether they have any questions regarding their upcoming surgery. This is a good time to review the admission procedures.

- A comprehensive educational seminar may be held days before or on the morning of surgery.

Making it work

Preadmission phone calls

Before admission, patients who will be receiving common procedures at Thomas Hospital receive a video. This video walks through the unit, surgery, and recovery and even introduces the nurses. Preadmissions calls each patient ahead of time to ensure that he or she has viewed the video and offers to answer any questions. Patients who have not viewed the video are flagged for educational counseling pre-surgery on the morning of admission, and this time is built into the schedule.

Best practice: Service protocols to elicit and address needs, existing and anticipated (Level IV)

Customer service protocols/standards ensure consistent delivery of services. A standard script or phrase designed to draw forth unvoiced concerns or desires will help ensure that all needs are met. Empathetically ask such questions as the following:

- *Are you in pain?* (If yes, follow through with standard pain assessment.)

- *Do you have any questions?*

- *Is there anything I can do for you?*

- *Is there anything that you're worried about?*

- *Do you have the medication you need?* (If no, obtain it for the patient, assuming that it's at the hospital pharmacy.)

- *Is there anything I can do to make you more comfortable?*

Intonation and nonverbal cues can help or hinder communication with patients. Practice and training in empathetic communication and standards will help staff become more confident and improve their use of these skills.

Note, however, that systematically eliciting patients' needs is not enough. Evidence shows that patients frequently are unaware of or uncertain about their future needs, especially postdischarge and pain-related needs. For example, in a study of patient expectations before planned elective surgery, patients were found to be unaware of

- the symptoms they would experience
- how to relieve those symptoms
- the potential of surgical complications
- fundamental process of care issues[1]

This and other studies prove what those working in healthcare see everyday: Simply helping patients and families understand the processes in a hospital is a huge task.

Likewise, patients typically do not have a clear understanding or expectation regarding pain.

     Patient Satisfaction and the Discharge Process

Although some, as mentioned earlier, expect their ailments to be cured, many expect to experience pain and often have low expectations for pain relief. This presents an opportunity for the hospital to exceed expectations. Further, patients often do not realize the extent to which basic, everyday activities depend on their mobility and freedom from pain and fatigue. Simply put, many patients don't know what questions to ask to get the information they will need and want down the road. Great service includes helping patients and families ask the right questions.

It also includes *anticipation*. Staff must know ahead of time the needs of patients and families and design a system to meet those needs with the right information (or service) at the right time. Patients will only feel ready to be discharged if you help them arrive at that conclusion with seamless service that anticipates their needs.

There are other protocols that will help address patient pain needs as well:

- Administer an analgesic just before discharge to minimize pain in transit (e.g., even ibuprofen can be helpful)

- Note in assessments how patients plan to negotiate stairs, high beds, and other maneuvers that aggravate pain

- Include pain intensity scales in standard employee education materials for the patient (and test to ensure comprehension), educate patients on what levels of pain to expect, and instruct employees on the importance of swift and effective treatment of pain

2. The patient does not fully understand his or her illness

The prevalence of chronic disease and shorter hospital lengths of stay (LOS) increase the likelihood that the patient's illness will accompany him or her home after discharge. Understanding the illness and its effect on their lives and ability to function frequently percolates to the top of patients' minds. This spotlights the nurse and physician role as patient educator and emphasizes that education, preparation, and planning for the transition home should be ongoing and can never begin too soon.

Best practice: Ongoing assessments and fulfillment of patients' educational needs (Level IV)

Regularly schedule assessments of patients' educational needs by different hospital personnel at various intervals throughout the hospitalization. Use the initial assessment to determine what the patient wants to learn and whether any language barriers exist. Also note the patient's culture, religion, emotional barriers, motivation, and physical and cognitive limitations. Include this initial assessment with the clinical needs assessment and establish protocols so that patients meeting certain assessment criteria automatically receive appropriate educational materials. The assessment should follow patients in their medical chart, and it should include the family's needs as well. Subsequent assessments should be frequent but less formal.

When assessing patient and family education needs, remember that everyone's learning style is unique. Staff at Thomas Hospital in Fairhope, AL, perform educational assessments that ask patients for their preferred learning method (e.g., reading, one-on-one instruction, video, audiotape, participatory, lecture, etc.) and deliver discharge instructions accordingly. For example, too much information at once can be confusing to a patient who is less cognitively adept, so assessment and inquiry at regular intervals work better for him or her.

Also note that a given patient's needs and desires for information fluctuate throughout the hospitalization experience. For example, a patient may want mass quantities of information before surgery, but postsurgery, that same patient may want to be left alone and reject all attempts to educate.

The goal is to deliver information that patients need and want to know, when they need to know it. Use different kinds of education (e.g., oral, written, printed, video, or audio) to tell patients

precisely what to expect and how to care for themselves at home and at many stages. Amateur videos that role-play the events that will occur during the hospitalization, including the discharge process, are strong patient education tools. Hospitals promote these videos by playing them continuously on hospital education channels and by placing written reminders on meal trays and in newspapers.

Words that work

Keep it simple

Evaluate assessments, educational materials, and discharge instructions to ensure that messages are communicated simply and easily. Materials should be written at a fifth or sixth grade reading and comprehension level and should not include any unnecessary words. Never use medical vernacular. Use the following examples:

- Do not say *myocardial infarction* or *m.i.*
  Say *heart attack*

- Do not say *You may experience some itchiness under the inside of the plaster cast*
  Say *You may feel itchy from the cast*

 Patient Satisfaction and the Discharge Process

3. The patient does not feel capable of self care

Regimens for self-care or medication may be complex or entirely foreign to the patient. This may be the first time that he or she has had to follow a strict regimen (e.g., routinely clean a wound or walk with crutches/walker), and physical rehabilitation/therapy exercises and activities of daily living may be painful and a source of genuine concern for the patient. Any difficulties or complications that occur once patients have spent a week recuperating may influence their perception of whether they were ready for discharge and affect your patient satisfaction scores.

Best practice: Comprehensive discharge planning for as many patients as possible (Level I)

Patient satisfaction is maximized when the

- patient participates intimately and frequently in the discharge planning process

- process involves patients immediately upon admission

- family and additional caregivers are consistently involved

- patient and family are presented with choices

Comprehensive discharge planning not only improves patient satisfaction where readiness for discharge is concerned but also improves patient satisfaction with all other components of the discharge process: speed, instruction, and coordination. Patients benefit from the concentrated attention, in-depth analysis, coordination, and acknowledgement of future needs in the home. They consistently show their appreciation through improved patient satisfaction ratings across all four measures. Even patients with limited needs (both in number and intensity) report higher levels of satisfaction when they are involved in comprehensive discharge planning.

Talk with patients and family members about everything that will happen on the day of discharge to help them visualize it and establish realistic expectations. Patients and family members will take comfort in the knowledge that their needs have been thoroughly evaluated and anticipated. They will feel that the hospital has done everything possible to ensure a smooth transition.

Best practice: Confirm that the patient has acquired the skills/services necessary to manage at home (Level IV)

Handing the patient written instructions does not mean that learning has occurred. Patients will rarely request information or voice ignorance of a subject; patients typically attempt to "muddle through." Therefore, relying on patients to present learning needs is ineffective as both an educational and a patient satisfaction strategy. Educational interventions and final discharge-readiness assessments that include some procedure to ensure that learning has occurred, not only flags the patients who need additional attention (or a different instruction strategy) but helps reinforce the desired lessons for those who demonstrate understanding.

Scripted language can ensure that learning has occurred:

- Ask patients to repeat or show what has been taught to them:
    - *When are you going to take these pills?*
    - *Show me how you will do your exercises.*

- Follow up on educational materials with direct inquiry:
    - *What did you think of our video?*
    - *Do you have any questions?*

4. The patient has not seen a physician recently

Patients rely on physicians for comfort as well as for expertise. Physicians' judgments, attention, and consultation provide patients with reassurance that the correct decisions are being made. Therefore, without recent physician involvement in discharge, patients may doubt their readiness to leave the hospital.

Best practice: Physician provides closure (Level IV)

A physician's approval and praise can be immensely reassuring and satisfying for patients. A final consultation, even in brief, can put patients at ease and provide encouragement.

Create a protocol in which physicians stop at the rooms of patients being discharged to answer last-minute questions and wish the patients well.

5. The patient expected or feels that the illness warrants a longer stay

The previous experiences of family and friends can strongly influence patients' expectations. Unless clinicians intervene and reorient patients to help them understand the scenario for their hospitalization, expectations may vary widely. Patients may expect miracle recoveries and immediate freedom from pain—or they may expect an extended convalescence.

Best practice: Protocols to manage the patient's expectations regarding length of stay (Level IV)

To pay explicit and respectful attention to managing patients' expectations for LOS, first discern patients' thoughts in this regard. At specific or multiple predetermined points along the hospitalization continuum, physicians, nurses, discharge planners, and social workers should tap into patients' perceptions of their goal (or what they would consider appropriate) LOS. Shorter LOSs and early discharges from the hospital do not necessarily negatively affect patient satisfaction—the perception of the experience makes all the difference.

Establish language protocols to communicate LOS-related issues in a respectful and considerate manner. Never say, *Medicare won't pay, so you have to leave"* or *"Your insurance doesn't cover you staying here any longer,"* as these statements convey that the patient is being kicked out earlier than the hospital and medical team feel is appropriate. Instead, say, *"We welcome your presence here at the hospital and enjoyed your stay with us, but the time for your discharge* [will be x date/has arrived]." Set up interactions with patients to determine their views regarding LOS, and respond to them in a kind and respectful way that meets their needs. The sooner that an accurate estimate for LOS is established, the better.

Making it work

Upfront LOS

Patients who enter Lexington Medical Center in West Columbia, SC, learn their expected LOS upon admission. Staff update this information as necessary, and for patients whose admissions are unexpected, staff quickly determine the expected LOS. The goal is to create the perception that all patients are discharged in a normal LOS given their condition.

6. The patient fears that something will go wrong now that he or she is away from expert care

Emotional distress is common during and after discharge. Patients may fear that the intense pain just experienced will return, the illness will regain control, complications will occur, or an accident will happen once they are separated from the sup-

port and care of nurses and other healthcare experts. For patients discharged home, the complete withdrawal of expert support is a common source of apprehension. For patients making the serious transition to a nursing home or some other facility, fears of the unknown, mistakes, neglect, and lack of comfort may supersede these concerns. Regardless of the situation, however, almost all patients and family experience some level of concern related to continuity of care.

Best practice: Contact information sheet (Level IV)

Something as simple as providing the patient with names and numbers of staff who can answer questions and talk them through their self-care will mitigate fears by providing the patient with explicit reassurance.

7. The patient/caregiver experiences emotional distress on the day of discharge

As mentioned before, the discharge phase is often riddled with emotions. Patients feel vulnerable and apprehensive. The elderly may be reluctant to transition to a long-term care facility or to their home, where they may be dependent on the care of others. The patient may feel frustrated with his or her weakened condition. Given these issues, it is easy to see how distressed emotions can be amplified for the discharged patient left to wait alone in the lobby, or when a last-minute patient and family concern is treated dismissively.

Best practice: Customer service or behavioral standards (Level IV)

Many hospitals implement overarching customer service standards or behavioral standards. When combined with leadership support, modeling, and intense employee involvement in development and administration, setting behavioral standards usually improves patient satisfaction and service quality. Likewise, behaviors exemplifying excellent customer service for the final day of the hospital stay can be identified and implemented by members of the healthcare team. Integration into daily practice calls for codification, leadership support, hiring and training for these standards, behavioral reinforcement, and accountability. Near limitless possibilities exist for customer service behaviors to enhance the experience of leaving the hospital and minimize emotional distress:

- Never leave patients alone once they have left their room for good

- If the patient is being discharged to another facility, call that facility the morning of to ensure that everything is ready

- Never force the patient to ride in a wheelchair

- Have volunteer(s) available solely to run last-minute errands and requests for patients or families

- Install a concierge service to accompany the patient and to carry his or her belongings (see Chapter 6 for more about concierge services)

- Hand out vouchers for free meal or gift shop items for patients and family to take advantage of on their way out

Something to think about

Most hospitals already have behavioral standards in place, but actually following through with them is the key to their success. It's easy to pay lip service to standards and values, but it's difficult to tell whether 100% of associates are acting out the standards 100% of the time. Achieving this level of consistency is what separates the 50th percentile from the 95th percentile—the good from the great.

8. The patient feels lack of control in the process; information needs remain unmet

Simply put, patients want to exert some level of control over their healthcare. Although the level of involvement a patient would like in treatment decision-making varies, all patients want to be involved in their future on the day of discharge.

 Patient Satisfaction and the Discharge Process

Best practice: Techniques for enhancing the patient's perception of involvement (Level IV)

Throughout the discharge planning process, patients and families must make all decisions. The role of the discharge planner, social worker, case manager, nurse, and other health professionals is to present all possible options and offer advice. The professional should never decide for the patient or portray the options in a way that is inherently limiting. Even if the professional thinks that a service or community resource is not a good option for the patient, he or she should still present it. For example, you could say, *This option may not fit your needs, but you should be aware of it.*

Throughout the literature about patient-perceived involvement in discharge planning, the most consistent theme is that healthcare providers must provide patients and families with time to think about their options. The sooner the patient and family have postdischarge options for serious consideration (ideally, prehospitalization for elective surgery), the better for patient satisfaction.

Next, think beyond patients' involvement in major decisions—examine all the small decisions that get made throughout the patient's stay as well. It is more than a little inconsistent to empower patients with the big decisions yet disable them from minor decisions, such as when they will eat, what they will eat, when they can sleep without interruption, the extent of their mobility, etc. Therefore, encourage patients and family members to take an active role in their care. Move toward creating a hospital experience that mirrors the real-world experience patients will soon re-enter. For example, some patients prefer to use the bathroom toilet instead of a bedpan. It may take extra time and effort to help patients to the bathroom, but this is the situation they will have to deal with at home. If there are no safety or medical concerns, give patients as much control over their care as they can handle.

On the actual day of discharge, take steps to ensure that the patient feels involved and in control. Subtle language and behaviors can make a palpable difference in patient perceptions. For example, don't say,

Mrs. Smith, it's already 1:15 p.m., and the time for your discharge was 1:00. You need to get your belongings together; we need this room.

Such an approach makes it sound like the patient is being kicked out. Instead, say,

Mrs. Smith, how are you doing? Let me help you organize your belongings so we can get ready to go. We don't want to keep your [son, daughter, parents, doctor, friends at x facility] *waiting.*

How you say things matters. Ask permission before doing anything that directly involves the patient, such as packing. Empathic communication and customer service behaviors are skills that healthcare professionals can learn and that result in improved patient satisfaction.

Hospital causes

1. A bed shortage rushes the discharge process

For many facilities, goals for reducing LOS are measured in hours, not just days. The pressure to open up beds can sometimes be so intense that the needs of the patients currently in them are forgotten.

Best practice: Improve overall flow (Level IV)

Problems in flow can create vicious cycles and induce turf-war behaviors (e.g., hoarding or non-communication). Delays, dissatisfaction, and other less-than-optimal outcomes can result. For example, improving the emergency department's (ED) overall patient flow time will free up ED beds. Patients waiting for admission can wait in the ED until the inpatient bed opens up, which prevents healthcare professionals from trying to rush patients out the door before everything is ready.

Patient flow problems are almost always systemic and require involvement and cooperation from multiple departments. Leadership commitment to focus quality improvement on patient flow is essential if you are to obtain full commitment from other parties. Specific causes vary; for example, resource needs (lack of resources or upgrades) may be part of the underlying cause. Whatever the cause, careful analysis by interdepartmental

team(s) and openness on the part of leadership to enable solutions is a requisite starting point.

Patient tracking systems and other support systems may be appropriate as well. Evidence shows that improving patient flow throughout the hospitalization process results in improved patient satisfaction with discharge.

Making it work

Stocking up on wheelchairs

As a rule at most hospitals, patients must be wheeled from their rooms to the door. At Lexington Medical Center in West Columbia, SC, a wheelchair shortage caused delays in patient discharges. Nursing units began to hoard and hide wheelchairs in closets and supply rooms, which only exacerbated the problem. Management responded by buying an exorbitant number of wheelchairs and "flooding" the units with them. The hoarding behavior ceased, and now patients can leave as soon as they are ready—no more waiting for a wheelchair.

---

2. Physicians, nurses, and specialists provided conflicting information about when the patient could go home

An inconsistent message on the expected discharge date indicates to patients and families a lack of team coordination and communication. "When can I go home?" is a common question that patients and family will ask everyone: the head nurse, specialist, primary care physician, discharge planner, etc. Conflicting answers chip away at patients' and family members' confidence in the quality of care at your hospital.

Something to think about

Never exaggerate the expected discharge date only to discharge the patient substantially earlier than previously stated or with little warning. The patient probably won't feel pleasantly surprised but instead will worry that he or she is not ready to leave the hospital.

Best practice: White board with expected discharge date (Level IV)

For the benefit of both the patients and members of the care team, many hospitals have installed white boards that list the patient's name, list the patient's nurse and technicians for the shift, list planned activities for the day, and provide space for the patient and family to write questions and comments. Noting/writing the estimated discharge date on this white board is one method hospitals have used to keep patients and all personnel aware of the anticipated date.

Making it work

A ticket to go home

In March 2004, staff at Virginia Mason Medical Center (VMMC) in Seattle decided that there was a better way to keep patients and families informed and engaged with the discharge planning. They decided that patients in VMMC's Acute Care for the Elderly (ACE) unit would receive a Ticket Home—a white laminated board placed in front of each patient's bed (see Figure 2.3). In large permanent black letters, easily seen by aging eyes, the 6 ft. x 2.5 ft. boards display all the fundamental questions about an individual's progress. At the top is a request for the projected date and time of discharge. Below are queries about specific requirements for leaving the hospital, such as whether a patient can eat and go to the bathroom alone, whether he or she can walk safely, the status of pain control and lab work, and whether safety risks have been addressed.

As the answers become available, medical staff, patients, and families can write on the board with colored markers, creating a fuller picture of the patient's current status than any one participant is likely to have alone. For instance, a patient can confirm that his pain has been brought under control with oral medication, a family member can announce that a ride home has been arranged, and a nurse can verify that lab tests are complete.

Sample ticket home

Ticket Home

Projected discharge date: _____

Time: _____

Patient milestones:

☐ I can feed myself _____

☐ I can toilet myself _____

☐ I can walk safely _____

☐ My pain is controlled on oral meds _____

☐ Medical goals met (labs, etc.) _____

_____

_____

Discharge goals/needs:

☐ I can walk safely around my house

☐ Safety risks addressed

☐ Learning needs met

☐ Ride home arranged/time:

If you have any questions or concerns, please ask your care team.

Tickets home provide information at a glance. There's room on one side of the board to list the day's scheduled tests and procedures and plenty of blank space for back-and-forth communication in the off-hours. Families can write questions and comments or leave instructions about a patient's preferred routines. Staff can reply in the same convenient spot, and everyone is assured that his or her messages won't get lost. An attached bulletin board with push pins invites visitors to post get well-cards or encouraging thoughts.

 Patient Satisfaction and the Discharge Process

3. There is no opportunity for gradual recovery and extended consideration of postdischarge options

The lines between nursing home, assisted-living, home health care, family care, and complete independence are not black and white. The decisions involved, especially for nursing home and assisted living, can be burdensome. Coming to a final decision can be especially difficult while still recovering in the hospital.

Best practice: Step-down unit (Level IV)

Through partnership with a long-term care or assisted-living facility, create a convalescence or step-down unit where elderly patients, after leaving the hospital, may spend two to four weeks before being discharged to their homes, an assisted living facility, or a nursing home. Work closely with physicians, who may recommend the unit to patents who may benefit from it. Awareness among primary care physicians could serve the same purpose and help plan for discharge arrangements before hospitalization.

To move to the step-down unit, patients' functional levels should

- be medically stable with minimal treatment

- be independently ambulatory

- be able to care for themselves relatively well

- require nursing care for assistance with

activities of daily living and supervision only

- not include any severe mental illness or other conditions (e.g., addiction) that might lead to noncompliance

This "semi-retirement" unit functions much like a lodge (with shared kitchen, etc.) and allows patients time to make decisions about their future in a safe, comforting environment where clinical expertise and assistance is immediately at hand.

4. Standard discharge procedures are not patient-centered

Forcing the patient and family to adhere to certain procedures, walk around the hospital to visit different departments, or make stops on the way home can create or add to the stress and frustration on the day of discharge.

Best practice: Examine day of discharge processes for possible redesign (Level V)

Map the processes related to leaving the hospital. Walk through the discharge process from the perspective of the patient, and redesign the process to make the patient's experience of leaving the hospital as effortless as possible. Try to keep the patient and family from having to make multiple stops either in the hospital or on the way home. Realize that tests on the day of discharge can be stressful. Make all activities for the day clear and explicit. If changes or delays occur, keep the patient continually updated; provide reasons, reassurance, and comfort; and continue to be open to fulfilling their personal needs.

Making it work

Mystery shoppers

At East Alabama Medical Center in Opelika, AL, mystery shoppers report back on facility performance. They delve into every facet of the organization, including human resources and other support functions.

The discharge-related procedures often are contingent on the physician discharge order. Nothing is done to prepare the patient until an order is given, and the patient sits until then. However, once the order is given, a flurry of activity ensues. Make a difference by preparing patients for discharge, as much as possible, before the order is given. Talk to them and their families; don't let them wonder what is happening. Tell them what you are waiting for and when you think it will occur. Offer to help patients by asking whether they would like anything.

5. There is no customer service procedure designed to impress patients as they leave

The final opportunity to create a positive impression with the patient or assuage a negative experience occurs at discharge.

Best practice: Make leaving the hospital a memorable event (Level IV)

Consider ways to send the patient off that will generate good feelings about their stay. Warm goodbyes with sincere thank yous (e.g., *Thank you for letting us take care of you* and *Thank you for staying with us*) are standard practice in the best hospitals.

Making it work

Thank you cards

Beginning with admissions at Lexington Medical Center in West Columbia, SC, a thank you card that expresses appreciation to patients for choosing the hospital as their provider is circulated with each patient. Every nurse who cares for the patient along the way signs it. All nurses sign the card with their full name and the department in which they work. The card is handed to the patient at discharge with a sincere, scripted "thank you." Not only is the patient usually surprised and pleased by the gesture, it also has the side effect of improving patients' ability to recall specific nurses' names on the survey. See Appendix C for sample language in a thank you card.

Other methods to impress patients as they depart vary. Some hospitals give patients a tote bag for their belongings. The bag displays the hospital logo and becomes a walking advertisement.

Patient Satisfaction and the Discharge Process

Other hospitals give patients and families meal vouchers to use in the cafeteria as they leave. Balloons, flowers, small gift certificates to the hospital gift shop ($2–$5), or other small tokens of appreciation are presented. Concierges and valet parking are always a welcome relief, reducing the anxiety and stress involved for patient and family.

The key to the success of each of these practices is a sincere, warm approach. With the right attitude, staff can impress the patient with sensational service.

Conclusion

As badly as patients may want to go home, many fear what could happen without the direct care of your excellent medical team. To alleviate this fear, do your part to make patients feel like they're ready to go home. The process you design for discharge and the actions of hospital staff in that process can either affirm or negate the patients' belief that they will be ready for it. Key best practices for communication, be it verbal (e.g., physician making room visits to ask whether there are any questions and using scripted language that doesn't make the patient feel rushed), written (e.g., a white board or Ticket Home), or intuitive (e.g., managing patients' expectations of discharge or knowing when to give the caregiver more information), all work toward improving patients' perceptions of their readiness for discharge.

References

1. Artinian 1991; Jones, Densen & Brown 1989; Jones, Burney & Christy 2000; Kemper & Mettler 2002; Lithner & Zilling 2000.

2. E. W. Jones, P. M. Densen, and S. D. Brown, "Posthospital Needs of Elderly People at Home: Findings from an Eight-Month Follow-up Study," *Health Services Research* 24 (1989): 643–664; K. R. Jones, R. E. Burney, and B. Christy, "Patient Expectations for Surgery: Are They Being Met?" Joint Commission Resources June (2000): 349–360; M. Lithner and T. Zilling, "Pre- and Postoperative Information Needs," *Patient Education and Counselling* 40, 29–37.

Speed of the discharge process

Learning objectives

By the end of this chapter, you should be able to

- identify potential patient causes for patient dissatisfaction with speed of the discharge process

- review best practices designed to address these root causes

- describe two things hospitals do to cause patient dissatisfaction with the speed of discharge

- describe the case facilitation philosophy and how it can enhance patient flow

- review best practices designed to address these root causes

3.1 FIGURE

Cause and effect fishbone diagram for speed of the discharge process

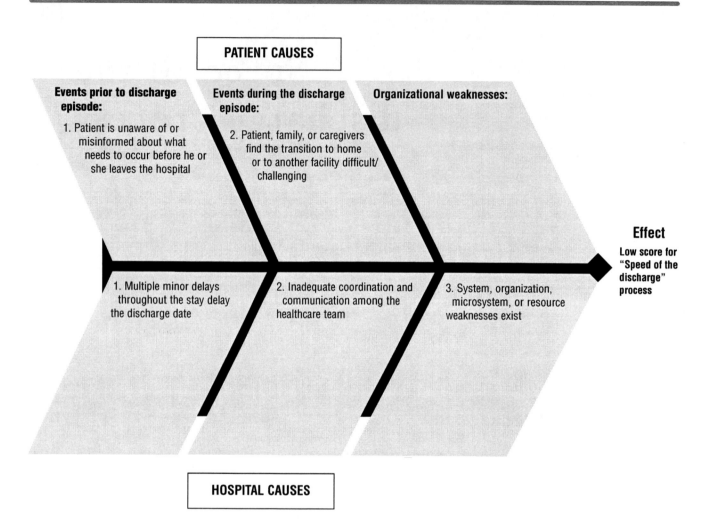

PATIENT CAUSES

Events prior to discharge episode:

1. Patient is unaware of or misinformed about what needs to occur before he or she leaves the hospital

Events during the discharge episode:

2. Patient, family, or caregivers find the transition to home or to another facility difficult/ challenging

Organizational weaknesses:

Effect

Low score for "Speed of the discharge" process

1. Multiple minor delays throughout the stay delay the discharge date

2. Inadequate coordination and communication among the healthcare team

3. System, organization, microsystem, or resource weaknesses exist

HOSPITAL CAUSES

 Patient Satisfaction and the Discharge Process

3.2 FIGURE	**Summary of best practices**

Level I	
Level II	• **Compress length of stay through case facilitation**
Level III	• Transition coordinator
Level IV	• **Structures to enhance and encourage communication**
Level V	• **Case managers round daily** • **Standardization of day of discharge events and streamline processes** • **Expand case management/social work services; rigorous hiring and performance standards**

Best practices in bold are those validated by original qualitative reseach conducted by Press Ganey. For information on the levels, see Table 1.3.

Speed of discharge measures patients' *perception* of the length of time it takes to physically leave the hospital after they are told they are being discharged. Although many patients remark that the discharge process takes too long, they often don't know all the steps that are involved in the process. Educating patients and their families or caregivers about the steps in the process will reduce patients' anxiety and frustration. It will also improve their perception of the value of the services provided as they begin to understand what is being done on their behalf.

Our qualitative studies of the most-improved and highest-performing hospitals for patient satisfaction with speed of discharge found a zealous focus on reducing the length of stay (LOS). Although prior studies did not find a strong relationship between patient satisfaction and LOS, our study with the largest national database found that patients were most satisfied with short

stays. Thus, decreasing LOS may be effectively leveraged as an organizational indicator of quality. This presents hospitals with an opportunity to improve patient satisfaction and hospital finances simultaneously.

Unfortunately, you can't improve patient satisfaction with the speed of discharge simply by doing whatever it takes to "street" patients. Satisfaction with speed of discharge depends on both *how quickly I can go home and how I'm cared for on the way*—which requires effectively attending to the needs of patients and managing their perceptions before and throughout the discharge process. For example, imagine the frustration of a patient who is told she can "go home tomorrow" only to find out that "tomorrow" means 5:00 p.m., when the admitting physician does rounds. Establishing and reinforcing an accurate understanding of the discharge process is just as important as having an efficient process.

Patient causes

1. The patient is unaware of or misinformed about what needs to occur before he or she leaves the hospital

The series of events that occur on the day of discharge can be complex and confusing and patients often don't speak up when they have questions or need informtion repeated. Patients and their families may experience several spells of waiting or uncertainty throughout the process:

- Waiting for a test in the morning

- Waiting for the results in their room

- Waiting for the doctor to review the results and confirm/write the discharge order

- Waiting for information on home care or medical equipment

- Waiting for transportation

The complexity of the process and chance for a breakdown in it increases with the number of steps and the external agents involved (e.g., home health agencies, medical transport, nursing homes). Coordinating with the latter can be most difficult to manage because more elements are out of the hospital staff's direct control.

Best practice: Case managers round daily (Level V)

Every morning, make sure that case managers/ social workers update each of their patients on everything that they are doing, reassess patients' discharge and postdischarge needs, and connect families and nursing staff. The higher the percentage of patients receiving the services of case managers/social workers, the greater effect the practice will have.

Simply put, patients and family need to know what is happening. If the patient's situation is complex enough to warrant the attention of case management, then it is also complex enough to warrant increased communication. Daily rounding also benefits case managers because the increased interaction improves the chances of uncovering new or previously unmentioned issues. Case managers need to tell patients what

- they plan to do before they do it. Give the patient options, and confirm that the discharge plan or other arrangements are aligned with the patients' wishes.

- is "in process" or currently being worked on and when completion is anticipated.

- has been done, the results, how the results affect the patient and/or family, and what can be done if the situation changes. For example, tell the patient: *Home care arrangements have been made for delivery of an oxygen tank. If something changes and you need additional arrangements or decide to cancel, here is who you need to contact.*

Making it work

Approximating departure time

"You can go home today, but it will take about five hours to complete everything that needs to be done, such as finishing your medical orders, receiving discharge instructions from your primary care nurse, and removing your IV."

"You can go home tomorrow. When I am here tomorrow at 6:00 p.m. for my rounds, we will begin the discharge process. The discharge process will take some time because we will need to finish your medical orders, remove your IV, and give you your discharge instructions."

When a physician tells a patient that he or she can go home tomorrow, the primary nurse could manage the patient's expectations by saying, *When your physician does rounds tomorrow at 2:00 p.m., you will most likely go home.* Or, *When your physician is here at 2:00 p.m., we will begin the discharge process, which will include* [fill in with discharge activities]. *This will take approximatly* [fill in with estimated time].

2. Patient, family, or caregivers find the transition to home or to another facility difficult/challenging.

Family members and caregivers usually are present at discharge. Typically, they have rearranged their lives (e.g., work, children, and other responsibilities) to be with the patient during discharge and to take him or her home, and they don't want to be kept waiting any more than the patient does. Also note that, depending on the patient's condition, the caregiver may be the one who fills out the patient satisfaction survey. Always make sure that the caregiver is informed of the discharge process and receives communication throughout.

Best practice: Standardization of day of discharge events and streamline processes (Level V)

Establish a universal time for discharge (most hospitals using this practice select 11:00 a.m. because it is before lunch but provides adequate time for preparations). Collaborate with physicians to ensure a standard discharge round at 11:00 a.m. Case managers, social workers, and nurses must prepare everything for the universal discharge time, so when the physician writes the discharge order, everything has already been prepared and patients are free to leave immediately.

If a universal discharge time is not viable, another option is to schedule a specific discharge appointment for each patient. Scheduling discharges was recently chosen as one of the

Making it work

Physician participation

Physician participation is critical to keeping a strict discharge time. Physicians at Greenwich (CT) Hospital used to round at different and unpredictable times. Nurses communicated to them the importance of a single discharge time. They described to the physicians how all equipment, education, paperwork, and transportation would be in place before they round; how earlier rounds would help the patient and family by reducing uncertainty and ambiguity; and how it would improve patient flow by opening up beds earlier. Physicians agreed and now always round during morning hours.

Institute for Healthcare Improvement's *Ten Powerful Ideas for Improving Patient Care*.[1] Scheduling an appointment ahead of time eliminates the typical mad scramble to get everything done after the doctor's discharge order is written. This concept is enacted in just a few steps:

1. Build an appropriate number of discharge appointment slots for each day based on the average number of patients discharged from that unit per day.

2. Adjust these slots based on the average number of discharges by day of the week, as certain days may be more intensive than others. For example, limited services on

Saturday and Sunday reduce the likelihood of discharge in internal medicine on those days (Figure 3.3). On the other hand, neonatal intensive care units tend to have a preponderance of discharges on the weekend (24%).[2] Clearly, adjustments should be made based on each unit's own data. Take the next step in reducing LOS by scheduling discharges on the weekend, when medically appropriate, if your data indicate variation favoring weekday over weekend discharges. Increasing weekend discharges frees up beds for emergency admissions over the weekend.

3. Assign discharge appointments for each patient as soon as possible. Elective surgery patients may be assigned discharge appointments during the preadmission process. Medical patients can be assigned appointments as soon as reasonable predictions can be made. Hospitals often have separate systems for medical and surgical patients, but all patients should receive an appointment at least 24 hours in advance.

4. Display the discharge appointment date and time prominently in the patient's room, and display a schedule of all discharges at the nurses' and physicians' workstations.

5. Schedule only one patient per slot. Doing so allows for a more evenly distributed

Patient Satisfaction and the Discharge Process

work flow throughout the day. Nurses may prefer this to having a large number of patients discharged at the same time.

6. Schedule transfers exactly as you would schedule the discharge.

7. As an indicator of success, track the percentage of patients actually discharged within 30 minutes of the discharge appointment time. The goal should be 100%.

Whether you choose a universal discharge time or scheduled discharges, streamlining the discharge process has numerous benefits for nurses and other hospital staff. Knowing the date and time of discharge allows for one to three days to complete work rather than a few hours. This knowledge gives everyone a modicum of control and predictability in his or her work, as well as a clear goal toward which to work. It reduces bottlenecks, improves patient flow and satisfaction, and is simple to understand and implement. In addition, staffing can be ramped up quickly to deal with large fluxes of patients.

3.3 FIGURE **Admissions and discharges for internal medicine**

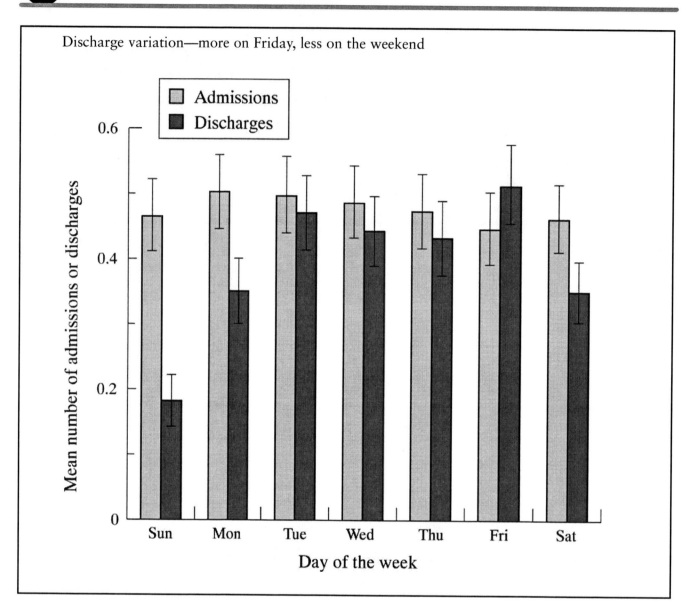

Discharge variation—more on Friday, less on the weekend

When the patient causes the delay

Although many patients want to leave immediately upon hearing that they can go home, not all of them do. Some patients may have scheduling issues with their loved ones, want to wait until after the next meal or fail to call their family until the last minute. Many other impediments (patient- or hospital-caused) may emerge as well. Greenwich Hospital organized a continuous quality improvement team, composed of all disciplines (e.g., food service, housekeeping, physicians, nurses, therapists), to brainstorm potential impediments to patients leaving promptly. Then they devised strategies to resolve each impediment and

      Patient Satisfaction and the Discharge Process

standardize universal events. By removing as many steps and roadblocks from the process, they were able to reduce LOS and increase patient satisfaction with the speed of the discharge process.

Transportation

Transportation from the hospital is another universal event that can benefit from a standard approach. Universal discharge time or scheduled discharge appointments eliminate ambiguity regarding when, but the question of who will provide the transport remains unanswered. Establish "Who will be taking you home at discharge?" as a standard question upon admission to address the issue, prepare the patient, and notify case managers/social workers of which patients need to resolve the issue.

Best practice: Transition coordinator (Level III)

A transition coordinator can ensure that all activities on the day of discharge occur smoothly. He or she reviews the day's schedule with the patient, family, charge nurse, physicians, receiving facilities, and transportation personnel. The transition coordinator also proactively reviews the discharge instructions, obtains additional educational materials, gathers information about medications, informs families ahead of time of their duties (e.g., transportation, prescription procurement), and serves as a resource throughout the final day. In addition, the coordinator identifies and mediates staff and facility problems and miscommunications before they reach the patient and family.

Spreading the message

Once standards are initiated, teach patients and family what to expect. Note the discharge time in all printed materials, on walls, on TV, on medical records, and verbally from nurses and case managers. Continuous communication and reinforcement of the same information from multiple parties will reduce ambiguity and concerns while comforting patients and family. Providing a consistent message enhances perceptions of quality.

Making it work

Discharge videos

A multidisciplinary group of employees at Banner Thunderbird Medical Center in Phoenix, AZ, produced a discharge video titled "Leaving the Hospital."

The seven-minute tape plays on the hospital patient education channel around the clock for viewing by patients and families. The segments coincide with the four areas of discharge, and topics such as transportation home, care instructions, medications, and postdischarge rehabilitation needs are outlined and explained in easy-to-understand terms. The roles of the nurse, physician, social worker, and case manager are introduced. Patients are encouraged to contact staff early in their stay for consultation and assistance. Throughout the video, the focus is on preparing patients for discharge. The video shows patients that there is more to discharge than meets the eye and educates them on the entire process, from getting the orders written to getting the discharge summary.

Nursing and case management staff refer patients to the video as soon as they are admit

ted, and a reminder to patients and their families to view the video is printed on patients' meal tray placemats and newspaper wrappers. Other Banner Health System hospitals are now adopting or revising this video for use in their own facilities.[3]

Froedtert's Case Management Department, composed of registered nurses, case managers, and social workers, created a discharge video that plays 24 hours a day on one of the education channels in the hospital. To gain high viewership, contests reward the units at this Wauwatosa, WI, hospital with the highest viewership. Nurses, PCAs, and other staff encourage patients to watch the video. Social workers and case managers who round every day with the doctors and nurses also encourage patients to watch the video.

And the information in the video is also included in the facility's *Planning for Your Discharge* booklet. Some units have even made signs for beneath the TV in the patient rooms that tells patients about the video.

 Patient Satisfaction and the Discharge Process

Hospital causes

1. Multiple minor delays throughout the stay delay the discharge date

Quality improvements that redesign grossly inefficient processes and procedures are important. More frequently, however, the problem is processes that are minutely inefficient, with slight delays or inefficiencies in the delivery of treatments, tests, therapies, and educational interventions. These seemingly negligible delays sometimes compound each other, resulting in a slightly longer stay. And extrapolated over thousands of patients each year, these small delays project to monumental proportions.

Best practice: Compress length of stay through case facilitation (Level II)

Facilities that perform at high levels or are most-improved in patient satisfaction with speed of discharge almost universally measured LOS for common surgical procedures by days and hours. A group composed of case managers, social workers, or unit nurses that assumes responsibility for decreasing LOS through case facilitation or designing early discharge programs can make a big difference.

2. Inadequate coordination and communication among the healthcare team

Poor communication and lack of coordination consistently prove to be the most pervasive and frequent causes for problems in the discharge process. Communication and coordination among

Words that work

Case facilitation

Case managers at Metropolitan Hospital in Grand Rapids, MI, have adopted a philosophy by which they assume the responsibility for facilitating or streamlining patient stays within the hospital. The goal is to reduce LOS and improve the patient's experience of navigating the hospital's system of tests, treatments, therapies, counseling, education, etc.

Beginning at the first chart review, the case manager/social worker determines what the patient needs before she or he can be discharged and advocates on the patient's behalf (e.g., calls technicians or therapists to move up appointment slots, calls the lab to get test results back faster, calls physicians with the results, etc.). By navigating the patient through all the necessary steps more quickly, the patient may be discharged hours, sometimes days, faster.

Physicians appreciate the case facilitation model because it gets them the results they need more quickly. Patients appreciate receiving quality service and having a champion help them navigate the system better. Success on the part of the case manager means beginning at the first chart review and continuing until the patient is discharged.

multiple disciplines, departments, and external entities (e.g., physician, community services, nursing homes, home health agencies) present a challenge for any hospital. The key is to meet clinical needs, documentation requirements, educational needs, and patient and family needs, as well as to make arrangements for all final tests, transportation, support, and destination provisions. These steps cannot occur smoothly without frequent, diligent communication.

Best practice: Structures to enhance and encourage communication (Level IV)

At high-performing hospitals feature structures specifically intended to enhance and encourage communication among all involved in the discharge process:

- **Multidisciplinary morning meetings:** Every person involved in patient discharge (e.g., social workers, case managers, discharge planners, utilization nurses, patient educators) meets in the morning to review the patients being discharged that day, any potential difficulties encountered, and any patients or families with special needs. Dividing into unit- or specialty-based teams in large hospitals is advisable. Related disciplines, such as quality improvement, patient satisfaction, and administration/ management, should regularly participate in these meetings. The frequency of these meetings could vary, but they should occur three or five days per week.

- **Team huddle or morning bed huddle:** Unit staff take 10–15 minutes in the morning to review the discharges anticipated for that day and what is required for each to be successful. If more in-depth review is needed, relevant staff members gather for a morning "bed huddle" with the patient and family to review what is needed to get ready for discharge.

- **Weekly quality improvement meetings:** These meetings involve the same personnel as in the daily morning meetings but focus on how the process can be improved. The point of the meeting is to review outcomes/measures, design and follow-through on the implementation interventions to improve the outcomes.

- **Daily schedule:** For the patients' and care team's benefit, staff share a schedule of the patient's activities for that day (either circulated via printed sheet or written on the patient's white board).

- **Day-of-discharge coordinator/liaison:** The morning of discharge, this person contacts every person/entity involved with the patient to ensure that every aspect has been readied for the patient. This includes contacting the
    - primary care physician
    - nursing unit
    - ambulance/transportation

- physician responsible for discharge
- receiving facility
- physician in charge of receiving the patient
- family

Through this method, problems are anticipated, met, and overcome so that the patient and family never encounter an impediment.

3. System, organization, microsystem, or resource weaknesses exist

Many hospitals recognize that organizational/ management changes are required in order to achieve the desired levels of patient satisfaction, and some have instituted these changes to cope with demographic changes in their service area (e.g., a large influx of population, a sharp unexpected rise in population, etc.). Nevertheless, every hospital in the "most improved" sample addresses weaknesses at some level of the organization.

Best practice: Expand case management/ social work services; rigorous hiring and performance standards (Level V)

Shift the purpose of case management from counseling only those most in need (e.g., frail, elderly, special needs, family problems) to serving **every** patient. Expand the case manager/ social worker repertoire to include the following:

- Determining service needs
- Rounding daily
- Communicating frequently with patients and families
- Preparing all required resources and equipment 24–48 hours in advance
- Assessing continuously

This expansion usually requires hiring more case managers, discharge planners, social workers, or patient educators. It also sometimes means hiring support personnel (e.g., an information specialist or transition coordinator). Set high standards for employment and evaluation. Conduct peer interviews, and do not fill the position unless the entire team agrees on the candidate. When investments are made in human capital, return on investment is evidenced by more competent case managers who are capable of carrying larger caseloads and receive more positive patient comments. At high-performing hospitals in the discharge section, close to 100% of patients receive case management/social work/discharge planning services.

Numerous studies have shown that when patients receive case management attention as they develop care plans, discharge plans, and postacute care plans, both patient satisfaction and clinical quality outcomes consistently improve—particularly for more complex transitions.[4]

> ## Making it work
>
> ### Hiring with attitude
>
> Thomas Hospital in Fairhope, AL, insists on only hiring the best. All case managers are RNs, and they are evaluated on patient satisfaction discharge section scores, readmission rates, LOSs, and clinical expertise/judgment.
>
> *"Hiring for attitude" is our main focus, regardless of the nursing shortage. We want the staff to be as close to perfect as possible. Processes are easy, but finding the people is difficult. The actual people who do the work day in and day out make the difference. Anyone who comes into contact with the patient must be caring, empathetic, knowledgeable, and have the right attitude. Patient satisfaction measures and feedback from other nurses are part of the six-month evaluation. We do not hesitate to unhire a nurse if it is not working out. More frequently, nurses not meeting standards will unhire themselves because they do not want to be in such an environment.*

The following three tactics were used by high-performing hospitals to achieve the objective of increasing patient satisfaction with discharge via case management and social work:

- Advancing discharge services personnel beyond unit nurses. Despite diversity in structure, personnel, and organization of discharge-related care, high-performing hospitals consistently exhibit exceptional competence and organizational support for advanced discharge services personnel. Although the charge nurse or the nurse providing care for that shift is involved in discharge, he or she is not the principal coordinator of discharge planning, education, or postdischarge services. And although the position names and backgrounds differed, hospitals with exceptional patient satisfaction in the discharge process emphasize, support, and expand the discharge-related roles beyond unit nurses. Whether labeled patient education, case management, or discharge planning, hospitals strived toward a goal of 100% involvement in patient care for that role.

- Ensuring strong, competent leadership of case management and patient education. If case management, social work, and/or discharge planning are expected to improve the speed of discharge and patient satisfaction, they must work proactively with other departments to coordinate activities, facilitate the process, and rigorously evaluate and redesign systems. The leader of these groups must be a positive and assertive change agent. In Press Ganey's best-performing facilities, such highly effective leaders direct case management and patient education departments.

Improving performance in this area with lackluster department leadership is highly unlikely. Successful leadership intuitively understands the importance of patient satisfaction and manages using this and other metrics. In addition to change management, leaders are actively involved in supporting the case managers and patient educators. Leaders are invested in serving patients, frequently rounding and often handling cases themselves. Dynamic leaders who fluidly operate up, down, and across the organizational chart are invaluable.

- Placing accountability on case managers. Finally, additional resources and responsibility must be coupled with accountability. Case managers, social workers, or discharge planners can be held accountable for their performance in several quantifiable ways:

  - Patient satisfaction with the discharge section
  - Readmission rate
  - LOS
  - Percentage of patients who receive discharge planning services
  - Percentage of patients with utilization review
  - Peer review (e.g., 360-degree feedback or chart review/evaluation)

Making it work

Peer review

Each month at Metropolitan Hospital in Grand Rapids, MI, case managers and discharge planners peer-review each others' charts using a form. The information collected in these forms is put into a graphical chart form to show, as a group, what areas need attention.

Conclusion

Patient satisfaction with speed of the discharge process depends on

- relentless operational and process improvements to decrease LOS and speed up the actual discharge process

- managing patients' perceptions of the speed of discharge before and throughout the process of transitioning out of your facility

This chapter reviewed proven practices for accomplishing these objectives:

- Daily rounding by case managers

- Standardized day-of-discharge events and streamlined processes

- Transition coordinator

Chapter three

- Compressing the length of stay through case facilitation

- Structures to enhance and encourage communication

- Expand case management/social work services

- Rigorous hiring and performance standards

All of these boast the WIFM (What's In It for Me?) of improving the manageability of hospital staff workload. Even more heartening is the ability to use this as a critical leverage point for improving the bottom line by reducing LOS while simultaneously improving patient satisfaction.

References

1. J. L. Reinertsen and W. Schellekens. *10 Powerful Ideas for Improving Patient Care.* (Chicago: ACHE Press, 2005).

2. S. M. Touch and others, "The Timing of Neonatal Discharge: An Example of Unwarranted Variation?" *Pediatrics* 107, no. 1 (2001): 737–7. Erratum in: *Pediatrics* 108, no. 5 (2001): 1240, http://pediatrics.aappublications .org/ cgi/content/abstract/107/1/73.

3. T. Laughlin and R. Coolwell, Leaving the Hospital: Satisfaction with the Discharge Process. *The Satisfaction Monitor.* March/April 2002.

4. D. B. Preen and others, "Effects of a Multidisciplinary, Post-Discharge Continuance of Care Intervention on Quality of Life, Discharge Satisfaction, and Hospital Length of Stay: A Randomized Controlled Trial," *International Journal for Quality in Health Care* 17, no. 1 (2005): 43–51; E. A. Coleman, P. Mahoney, and C. Parry, "Assessing the Quality of Preparation for Posthospital Care from the Patient's Perspective: The Care Transitions Measure," *Medical Care* 43, no. 3 (2005): 246–255.

Patient Satisfaction and the Discharge Process

Instructions given about how to care for yourself at home

Learning objectives

By the end of this chapter, you should be able to

- explain why patients may feel helpless to care for themselves once they get home from the hospital
- indentify three ways in which you can help improve patients' education/instruction recall
- describe the role of the patient education nurse
- list two imvestments a hospital can make to improve the quality of patient education

Staff and patients often have different perceptions about the information that patients need. These instructions for self care may focus on

- dietary and treatment regimens
- medications and their side effects
- potential danger signs
- when to resume normal activities/return to work

4.1

Cause and effect fishbone diagram for discharge instructions

PATIENT CAUSES

Information/Content of discharge instruction:

1. Information and education delivered but not recalled by patient and family

Delivery/Quality of instruction and patient education materials:

2. Expectations are contrary to actual course of illness, hospital stay, postdischarge recovery, etc.

3. Poor learning ability, low literacy level, language barriers, different learning style, varied educational needs, etc.

4. Patient and/or family doesn't fully understand illness and/or condition

Failure to meet needs in the discharge episode:

5. Patient/family experience a loss of control/choice and disengage from decisions about postdischarge treatment, regimens, etc.

Effect

Low score for "Instructions for how to care for yourself at home"

1. Minimal information given and what is given is not relevant to the concerns of patient and family; fails to effectively address the paramount information and education needs

2. Educational materials/ instructions appear unprofessional, illegible, too complex, etc.

3. Educational materials ineffective; conflicting information; educational materials on patient's specific condition not available

4. Gaps in service on day of discharge leave patient/family uncertain as to what's happening, what's going on, etc.

HOSPITAL CAUSES

4.2 FIGURE   **Summary of best practices**

Level I	
Level II	• **Information repetition** • Professional translation (for non-English-speakers) • **Written information about risks, potential treatments, and medication side effects, symptoms management, pain management, follow-up, etc.** • **Unit-based case management**
Level III	• Comprehensive educational resources, materials, and delivery methods
Level IV	• **Multimedia take-home materials (e.g., color pictures, videotapes, audiotapes)** • Patient education nurses specialized in specific conditions • In-depth caregiver assessment and education • **Substantial investments in patient education (human and structural capital)**
Level V	• **On-demand and personalized patient education** • Demonstration of learning • Hardwire patient education to diagnosis
Mixed	• Clinical pathways

Best practices in bold are those validated by original qualitative reseach conducted by Press Ganey. For information on the levels, see Table 1.3.

Patients perceive and recall instruction based on its relevance to their needs and concerns. Therefore, involving patients and their caregivers or families in this process is critical to the success of patients' recovery.

One might hypothesize that education provided earlier in the hospital stay would influence patients' evaluations of "Instructions given about how to care for yourself at home." Analysis of this question confirmed that patients perceive this question to be distinct from information provided in earlier stages of the hospitalization. Only relatively mild correlations were found between patients' satisfaction with discharge instructions for care at home and measures of information

provision. Rank-ordering the relationships between individual survey items and the question regarding discharge instructions for care at home, "How well nurses kept you informed," ranked 10th; "Information given your family about your condition and treatment" ranked 14th; and "How well physician kept you informed" ranked 19th. This suggests that meeting patients' information needs throughout hospitalization will not necessarily result in satisfaction with discharge instructions for care at home. Again, discharge is experienced as a distinct episode. Thus, a health-care team may be proficient in providing patients and families with information throughout the hospitalization experience, but such efforts will not satisfy patients' needs across the continuum.

There are several patient and hospital causes for dissatisfaction regarding the topic of patient self-care.

Patient causes

1. Information and education delivered but not recalled by patient and family

Hospital staff and physicians deliver education, care instructions, and information on topics such as the interpretation of test results, changes in functional ability, and the effect of the patient's condition on activities of daily living. Any of these may fall under the rubric of discharge instruction. In this situation, there are two factors at work against your facility:

- A majority of patients and families cannot recall information received in the hospital when it is delivered using the standard methods.

- A vast discrepancy exists in doctors' and nurses' perceptions of patient and family information needs and the amount of information needed to satisfy patients and families.

Best practice: Information repetition (Level II)
In current practice, patients and family are given important information by physicians, nurses, or discharge planners, but unless patients specifically request it, this information will not be repeated. Healthcare professionals may perceive such repetition as excessive, but patients and families may find it reassuring, comforting, and more comprehensible. Examples of standardized processes that reinforce information include the following:

- Deliver information orally, and hand the patient the same information in a pamphlet, brochure, etc. Later, repeat the information and explicitly apply it to the patient, using his or her name and other personal identifiers.

- Case managers can read the medical record to find out what nurses, physicians, and patient educators have told the patients. They can then reinforce any education and instructions the patient has received.

- On the day of discharge, the physician writes the patient's discharge order and speaks with the patient. Nurses and case managers should be nearby to listen to what the physician instructs the patient (and reads the physician's instructions on a standardized sheet). After the physician leaves, the nurse or case manager immediately repeats the instructions in both oral and written form.

Words that work

Recall through demonstration

Patient educators at East Alabama Medical Center in Opelika, AL strictly adhere to a demonstration-of-comprehension standard on anything they teach the patient. This demonstration varies by subject, but most frequently, staff instruct patients to "show me." In addition, before admission, patients may receive items to practice in order to "master" the skills needed for discharge (e.g., sponge to prepare the skin, barometers to prepare the lungs, etc.).

Best practice: Multimedia take-home materials (e.g., color pictures, videotapes, audiotapes) (Level IV)

The value of detailed written information for patients to take home as reference is well established. Color pictures, instructional videos, and audiotapes that clearly portray the patient's condition help alleviate concerns. These materials humanize the illness and bring to life printed descriptions for self-care and symptoms that patients may have difficulty visualizing. Multimedia discharge instructions substantially improve patients' recall and compliance.

2. Expectations are contrary to the actual course of illness, hospital stay, postdischarge recovery, etc.

The vast majority of surgical procedures consist of predictable processes and actions. Although these processes may be well known to healthcare professionals, patients and families find the entire situation foreign and confusing. Take steps to establish what to expect and when to expect it— doing so will substantially reduce patients' and families' fear and anxiety.

Best practice: Clinical pathways (mixed)

Clinical pathways provide a system for establishing patients' expectations and a structure for communicating consistently with the patient. This system puts patients at Centra Health System in Lynchburg, VA, at ease because nurses, physicians, and all staff operate under identical guidelines/documentation. Standard educational interventions and services are scheduled for each day of the patient's stay, so the patient, family, and staff know exactly what to expect. This process virtually eliminates the need for referrals (for therapy, education, etc.) because the services are already scheduled to happen. Preoperatively, patients receive the schedule for their stay in oral and written form.

Something to think about

Evidence regarding the effect of clinical pathways on patient satisfaction is mixed. Most studies have shown no effect, and only a few show significant improvements.

Our qualitative research found a similar mix. Two hospitals considered clinical pathways critical to their performance in patient satisfaction, although of those two, Centra Health System needed three years to fully implement clinical pathways and observe changes in patient satisfaction and measures of clinical quality. In contrast, one hospital considered *eliminating* clinical pathways to be crucial to its improvement. This hospital instituted a structure for communicating and establishing patient expectations through stronger case management and 100% comprehensive discharge.

3. The patient experiences learning/ language barriers

The average patient and family simply do not have education or experience similar to that of a healthcare professional. Moreover, even a well-educated patient may not be familiar or comfortable with specialized medical terminology. Even seemingly simple regimes such as wound and plaster care must be thoroughly explained in easily understandable language. Communicating these regimes is even more difficult when patients and families speak a language other than English.

Best practice: Professional translation (for non-English-speakers) (Level II)

The saliency of this practice depends on the percentage of patients with language barriers your facility encounters. The existence of a language barrier (without translation services) conclusively shows a negative correlation with patient satisfaction. Satisfaction significantly improves when the hospital provides professional translation services. However, if the percentage of patients who need translators is small, the funds may be better spent on another initiative.

Something to think about

The use of nonprofessional translators, such as family members or ad-hoc translators, can actually result in lower patient satisfaction. It not only raises confidentiality issues, but serious medical errors are more likely in these situations. Evidence favors the use of professional translation services to improve patient satisfaction.

Telephone translation services have been shown to achieve the same level of patient satisfaction as professional translation services. The evidence does not favor one practice over the other.

 Patient Satisfaction and the Discharge Process

4. The patient or family doesn't fully understand the illness/condition

As patient expectations for services and amenities during hospitalization increase, so do the expectations for an educational experience. Patients place increased importance on active engagement in managing their health. This trend will continue to grow as the prevalence of chronic illness rises in our aging population.

Best practice: Comprehensive educational resources, materials, and delivery methods (Level III)

Leading hospitals have instituted a cornucopia of multifaceted patient education resources, resulting in improved patient satisfaction:

- Aesthetically pleasing "Patient and Family Education Centers" (typically located adjacent to the hospital lobby) are available to patients, families, and the community

- Videos and audiotapes about illnesses, recovery, and self-care

- Support groups or discussions led by former or current patients with a particular illness

- Bedside computers that can access the Internet and provide a virtual library, interactive simulations, and guides to online resources

All materials, videos, instructions, etc., should be tailored to a sixth or eighth grade reading and comprehension level. Patients and their families should be consulted in developing and testing of these educational interventions (through focus groups, existing support groups, or interviews). Each of these varied interventions has resulted in at least a minute increase in patient satisfaction for a particular hospital or unit.

To better meet your patients' needs during hospitalization, consider diversifying your format. For example, reading could be taxing on an elderly patient, but a video could be entertaining and relaxing. An increasing number of patients and family members want to be able to connect to the Internet either through hospital computers or their own laptops. A patient's awareness of, participation in, and positive experience with such resources are critical to success.

Especially with the prevalence of chronic illnesses on the rise, many hospitalized patients are not

Making it work

Customized multimedia services

At Greenwich (CT) Hospital, an interactive television system provides patients with access to the Internet, e-mail, patient education, premium movies, and television at the bedside.

This system also interfaces with a clinical information system and patient education videos. Nurses anywhere in the hospital can order an education video for a patient, and because the videos are digital, the nurse can create customized educational videos composed of clips tailored to the specific needs and education level of the patient.

The nurse generates these videos from his or her computer and assigns them to be delivered to the patient's room. At the end of each educational clip or video, short questions are asked to test comprehension. The answers are documented electronically. If the patient does not receive a passing score (80% correct), the nurse receives a fax notifying him or her that the patient did not pass and identifying the questions that were answered incorrectly. The nurse can then provide one-on-one teaching.

The hospital only charges the patient for the premium movie services ($9.99 for 24 hours of access to all movies), not for educational videos. Services are provided by the Get Well Network (*www.getwellnetwork.com*) for $300,000.

Something to think about

YIELD Greenwich faced challenges in implementing customized multimedia services:

- The patient education committee spent a substantial amount of time ensuring accuracy. The chief of each medical section reviewed the videos related to his or her expertise.
- Matching videos with the most common diagnosis-related groups for the hospital sometimes required considerable effort.
- The facility's television system network had to be replaced.

- Educating the nursing staff to encourage adoption and use took substantial time and effort before it became a component of daily practice.

Despite the challenges of implementation, Greenwich Hospital feels that the result was worth the trouble. The hospital scored in the 99th percentile in patient satisfaction with "Instructions given about how to care for yourself at home" and increased its mean score by almost 1.0 over six months after implementation.

 Patient Satisfaction and the Discharge Process

"cured" at discharge but rather face having to manage an illness for the rest of their lives. This prospect can be daunting. The education and information a hospital currently provides is unlikely to satiate a patient newly diagnosed with a chronic illness, let alone a patient who has lived with an illness for any length of time.

Best practice: Patient education nurses specialized in specific conditions (Level IV)

Expand the standard group of patient education nurses to include education nurses who specialize in common chronic conditions. Adding two to four nurses to educate patients in each of the following areas will serve patients' needs for indepth learning and serve as resident authorities for the entire staff:

- Cardiology
- Diabetes
- Stroke
- Cancer

If expanding patient education personnel is not feasible, have each patient education nurse select a specialty in which to gather information, create educational materials, and keep up to date on the relevant literature.

5. Patient/family experience a loss of control/choice and disengage from decisions about postdischarge treatment, regimens, etc.

Illness and hospitalization often mean a loss of control over one's health and life. Patients and families want desperately to determine their future beyond the hospital. They want to have a choice of postdischarge options at every level, from deciding whether a nursing home, assisted-living facility, apartment, or home would be the best environment based on the character and schedule of a rehabilitation regimen. They want to be presented with options, information, counseling, and advice. They do not want decisions to be made for them or forced on them by their insurance policy. Indeed, involvement in decision-making is one of the measures most highly correlated with patient satisfaction with discharge instruction.

Several factors underscore the importance of the primary caregiver's involvement in the process. First, healthcare surveys have a consistent, non-trivial proxy completion rate. In addition, primary caregivers even help the patient complete the patient satisfaction survey (which will arrive after the caregiver and patient have spent several days at home coping with convalescence, rehabilitation, and gradual resumption of normal activities). Most importantly, however, the care-giver (usually a family member) is critical to the patient. Many patients suffer immense emotional stress when they feel that they are "being a burden" or causing trouble for their family or loved ones. A postdischarge environment in which the caregiver struggles and finds him- or herself unprepared to handle the situation will cause both the patient and caregiver to question whether they were ready for discharge.

Best practice: In-depth caregiver assessment and education (Level IV)

Beyond standard procedures designed to assess the caregiver's capabilities to meet the medical, diet, and basic care needs of the patient, this approach intends to meet the caregiver's informational, emotional, and support needs. Caregiver needs include

- information about the illness

- information about what to expect as the illness progresses (or potentially progresses)

- special diets or health strategies that might benefit the patient

- education about fundamentals such as caring techniques

- meal preparation tips

- detailed information about symptoms (and

which symptoms warrant professional medical attention)

- pain management techniques (including nonpharmacologic techniques)

- community resources and support groups

Particularly in cases of extended home recuperation, the caregiver could benefit substantially from learning coping, time management, stress reduction, and personal health maintenance skills. Beyond the realm of skills and caring, consider the family's emotional readiness as a component of assessment and education. Carrying out an in-depth assessment often encourages substantial family involvement and input. Examples of family caregiver assessments are included in Appendix D.

Hospital causes

1. Information given is minimal and irrelevant to the concerns of patient and family; fails to address effectively the paramount information and education needs

Patients and families will not remember any information they do not consider important. During this period, they are wracked with their own concerns, fears, worries, and information needs. Given the strenuous context in which discharge instruction occurs, it should not be surprising that they rarely recall the contents of discharge planning conferences, teaching sessions,

 Patient Satisfaction and the Discharge Process

etc. This underscores the importance of soliciting patients' and families' unique needs.

Best practice: Written information about risks, potential treatment and medication side effects, symptom management, pain management, follow-up, etc. (Level II)

Patients want information about follow-up, home care, symptom management, pain management, and coping with potential health problems. They want specific written information and resources about follow-up and community services, pain treatment, and life activities (e.g., whether they can go grocery shopping). And although healthcare professionals may dismiss passing on information that seems obvious, patients want written information about risks and potential side effects, no matter how miniscule. Each of these pieces of information has been shown to improve patient satisfaction.

2. Educational materials and instructions appear unprofessional, are illegible, and are difficult to understand

Review your systems for delivering education and consider whether you fall short on any of the following questions:

- What educational resources are available?

- Are patients aware of resource availability?

- Are all healthcare team members aware of and able to obtain educational material for patients?

- How does education flow to the patient? Is a referral to a patient education department required? Do nurses consult books at the nursing station? Is there a central library?

- Does the typical method consist of a nurse photocopying a page from a book?

- Are materials
  - tailored to the patient's perspective with information about symptoms, pain, managing at home, etc?
  - presented in a brief, easy-to-read format and appropriate (fifth to sixth grade) reading and comprehension level?
  - interesting?
  - motivating?

- Have the educational materials undergone a validation study to ensure efficacy? (For example, are the intended messages actually reaching the patients? Do patients recall the information?)

Best practice: On-demand and personalized patient education (Level V)

Although the patient does not actually see the systems supporting the healthcare team, he or she does perceive and evaluate the outcomes of these systems. Patients can readily evaluate whether information is tailored to their needs, how quickly the nurses respond to their inquiries, whether they understand the information, and the

---

Making it work

Thomas Hospital in Fairhope, AL, uses a CPSI (Computer Programs & Services, Inc. [*www. cpsinet.com*]) computer database, which automatically refers patients to education nurses. Implemented in 1995, this database creates computerized, personalized discharge instructions for all patients. The system also automatically generates personalized patient education sheets to aid patients in areas such as wound care, activities for daily living, and future app-ointments for rehab/therapy. It makes all discharge information and education available in-stantly for the nurses, which helps speed the process and readily fulfill patient and family requests. The system is easily searchable and customizable should additional information be desired.

---

attractiveness of the educational material (e.g., a blurry photocopy versus a color print on thicker paper, personalized and illustrated).

The most satisfying educational materials make the reader feel good. For example, add motivational quotes or brief stories for inspiration. Hospitals experience increases in patient satisfaction with the addition of an information system that provides patient education on-demand (but always in conjunction with other interventions). Additional systems can automatically prompt team members to complete necessary tasks or assessments throughout the discharge process and to help ensure that patients are not overlooked or critical steps not taken.

3. Educational mater ials are ineffective, contain conflicting information, or don't exist for the patient's specific condition

A large part of discharge instruction revolves around caring for oneself after hospitalization.

Patients and families will be highly disappointed with service quality if detailed answers and in-depth education regarding their illness and condition are not readily forthcoming. Worse yet is when staff provide conflicting information—patients expect the hospital to be the leading expert on health in their community. Many hospitals want to assume this role (and may even promote themselves to this effect), but underserving the educational needs of patients and families at the most crucial juncture is not the way to earn it. These actions will be reflected in mediocre patient evaluations.

Best practice: Demonstration of learning (Level V)

The Joint Commission on Accreditation of Healthcare Organizations' (JCAHO) patient education standards require that patients demonstrate what they learn. However, it can be difficult to implement this protocol and make sure it is followed consistently. As mentioned earlier, have patient educators practice using the phrase,

"Now, show me." Make sure that nurses and educators reinforce this standard by requiring demonstrations of learning with a final demonstration on the day of discharge. Repetition and reinforcement improve the ability to recall instructions. The exact learning requirements will differ by subject matter, but best-performing hospitals aim for rigorous comprehension standards above those required by JCAHO.

Best practice: Hardwire patient education to diagnosis (Level V)

Standard operating procedures/standing orders for specific conditions and diagnoses automatically trigger the delivery of appropriate patient education materials. Information about condition, diagnosis, and/or surgery also may be given upon admission. Enable a broad set of personnel to deliver basic patient education materials.

Making it work

Preoperation education

Before patients come in for surgery at East Alabama Medical Center in Opelika AL, they view a video. This 10-minute presentation shows exactly where the patient is going to go, what his or her wounds will look like, etc. Patients may take this video home to review as needed.

Best practice: Unit-based case management (Level II)

Most-improved and highest-performing hospitals in our qualitative research sample and a randomized controlled trial agree that strong case management organization leads to optimum patient satisfaction. Assigning at least one case manager in each unit increases communication, coordination, and frequency of interaction with patients. Close proximity promotes serendipitous communication. Clear signage and a location convenient to patients and unit nurses encourage consultation and inquiry. Unit-based case managers often will round the unit daily to visit patients, assess needs, and offer assistance/service. This model often requires the expansion of case management to serve all patients, not simply those most in need.

Best practice: Substantial investments in patient education (human and structural capital) (Level IV)

The greatest leap in quality of education is made in the investment in quality of human and structural capital. Every high-performing or most-improved facility made a substantial dedication of resources. Examples include the following:

- Dedicate a group composed of superlative persons from multiple disciplines to devoting significant time and energy into evaluating and building the organization's patient education resources.

- Evaluate the effectiveness of patient education materials. Validate their effectiveness by conducting focus groups, obtaining feedback from former patients, etc. Make sure that the materials convey the intended message and are easy to understand.

- Expand the patient education department to a ratio of one patient education nurse for every 10 patients.

- Dedicate information specialists to support patient education and case management in delivery of quality information and education.

- Provide learning and professional development opportunities for case managers and patient educators. Quality improves by expanding their knowledge and abilities.

- Conduct continual organizational learning in both clinical knowledge and service skills (e.g., communication, teaching, etc.).

- Institute stringent hiring processes. Hiring only the best, most knowledgeable, and most experienced nurses to be case managers increases effectiveness and return on investment.

Making it work

Staff offices on unit floors

Case manager, discharge planner, and patient educator offices at Centra Health System in Lynchburg, VA, are directly on the unit, even though each of these employees works for different departments. This close proximity to the patients leads to more frequent contact. Patients and family are shown where the case manager's office is and encouraged to visit it if they have any questions, concerns, or needs. It also increases the frequency of communication and collaboration between these different disciplines and the nurses in charge of the patient's care.

Conclusion

Discharge instruction only achieves success when the right information gets communicated in a way that enables the patient and/or loved one to absorb that information, recall it at a later time, and enjoy the learning experience. Education itself is challenging enough, let alone in a stressful environment with physical discomforts. Many proven practices were discussed in this chapter which can help, especially if considered in the following hierarchy:

 Patient Satisfaction and the Discharge Process

First, obtain the resources—both content and human resources—for effective discharge instruction and patient education:

- Comprehensive educational resources, materials, and delivery methods

- Written information about risks, potential treatment and medication side effects, symptom management, pain management, follow-up, etc.

- On-demand and personalized patient education

- Patient education nurses specialized in specific conditions

- Substantial investments in patient education (human and structural capital)

Next, make certain those resources are understandable:

- Professional translation (for non-English-speakers)

- Multimedia take-home materials (e.g., color pictures, videotapes, audiotapes)

Then create, practice, and follow processes that ensure those instructions are transferred consistently and effectively. In other words, make certain that the delivery method is effective:

- Information repetition
- Demonstration of learning
- In-depth caregiver assessment and education
- Unit-based case management

Finally, make certain that this happens as frequently as possible. The goal is to ensure that 100% of patients receive formal, written discharge instructions. Sometimes hardwiring the discharge instructions to a diagnosis or clinical pathway improves patient satisfaction, but not always. However, as illustrated above, if the actual content is not informative or understandable, then the instructions won't be communicated effectively, no matter the process.

Arrangements for follow-up and home care

Learning objectives

By the end of this chapter, you should be able to

- identify potential hospital and patient causes for patient dissatisfaction with the hospital's arrangements for follow-up and home care

- review best practices designed to address these root causes

- indentify three questions staff can ask patients to elicit unspoken concerns or needs

- describe five basic living activities that patients will need to perform after discharge

- describe the potential effect of postdischarge callbacks and home visits on patient concerns about unanticipated needs arising postdischarge

5.1 FIGURE

Cause and effect fishbone diagram for arrangements for follow-up and home care

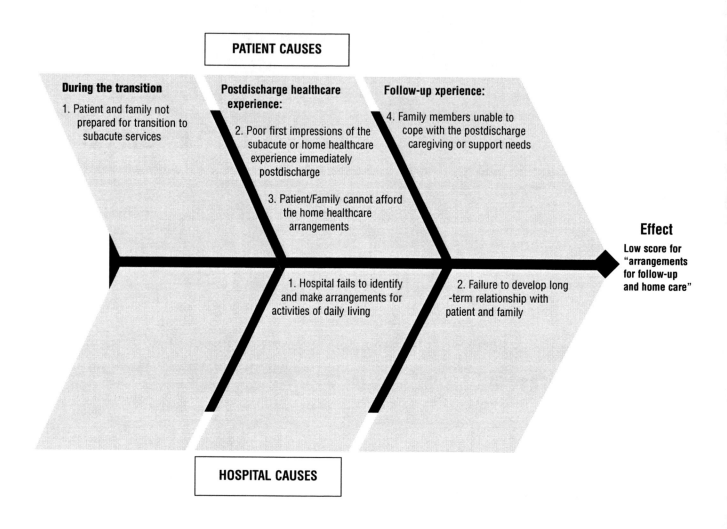

PATIENT CAUSES

During the transition

1. Patient and family not prepared for transition to subacute services

Postdischarge healthcare experience:

2. Poor first impressions of the subacute or home healthcare experience immediately postdischarge

3. Patient/Family cannot afford the home healthcare arrangements

Follow-up xperience:

4. Family members unable to cope with the postdischarge caregiving or support needs

Effect

Low score for "arrangements for follow-up and home care"

1. Hospital fails to identify and make arrangements for activities of daily living

2. Failure to develop long -term relationship with patient and family

HOSPITAL CAUSES

Patient Satisfaction and the Discharge Process

5.2 **5.2** FIGURE

Summary of best practices

Level I	**Postdischarge phone calls**
Level II	In-depth caregiver and family assessment and education
Level III	**Family meetings**
Level IV	Emotionally prepare patients and families for changes in their lives Evaluate the emotional experience of processes, eliminate stressors, and maximize positive emotions Cross-organizational or cross-departmental collaborative service quality improvement Check for financial obstacles and provide financial counseling Express to patients the importance of filling out the survey Recommend hospital, health system, or community resources
Level V	

Best practices in bold are those validated by original qualitative research conducted by Press Ganey. For information on the levels see Table 1.3.

The last hurdle to achieving a world-class discharge process is understanding that the patient's experience with your facility does not end when he or she walks out the door. All subsequent experience in postacute care, at home, and in transit reflect upon your institution. Patients will consider their hospitalization experience in the days after discharge and, good or bad, it will determine their evaluation of your coordination of care and teamwork.

Patients perceive the survey question regarding help arranging home care services as pertaining to all services, products, and issues related to their healthcare immediately following hospitalization. These perceptions are not limited to

traditional home health services. To understand the patient perspective, think broadly of all healthcare-related activities that may typically follow discharge:

- Medication acquisition and management

- Medical equipment acquisition, learning, practice, and use

- Rehabilitation activities (e.g., physical therapy, occupational therapy)

- Follow-up appointments for additional tests, for therapies, and/or with primary care/specialty physicians

- Adjusting/converting the home to enable daily living activities (ADL)

- Changing habits to accommodate new health realities

Patients' perceptions of the quality of these arrangements go beyond simply conducting need assessments and making arrangements. If the arrangements fall through, don't match patients' actual needs, or are of poor quality, patients will point the finger at your facility. Ultimately, achievement of high patient satisfaction and loyalty to your facility depend on these final impressions. Therefore, you have a vested interest in ensuring a successful patient experience

- in subacute care (e.g., rehabilitation, hospice, nursing homes, or other skilled nursing facilities)

- with postacute therapies or home healthcare

- at home

This final component of the discharge process may be the toughest to improve simply because the hospital does not control all the variables at play. Superlative performance in the patient's final care experiences necessitates working with people in other organizations to create mutually

beneficial processes for coordinating. To do so, first look at both patient and hospital actions and behaviors that can cause low scores on the follow-up and home care section of the patient satisfaction survey.

Patient causes

1. The patient and family are not prepared for the transition to sub-acute services

Moving patients to a new setting typically doesn't take long. Making arrangements to send and actually sending an 80-year-old patient to a nursing home may only take 60 minutes. But you're not shipping cargo. This is a human being with a life, a family, feelings, desires, and goals.

The best estimates available show that roughly one-third of all patients experience clinically significant levels of anxiety, depression, stress (including post-traumatic stress disorder), and/or other acute psychological problems. The causes of these negative psychological incidences lie not with the illness but rather with the experience of being in the hospital. And despite being treatable, these problems tend to be systematically ignored because the existing system for treatment is not readily available or easy to invoke. To conquer this, the objective is to create an easy and efficient system for detecting, assessing, and tailoring psychosocial interventions to patients' particular emotional needs.

Patient Satisfaction and the Discharge Process

Best practice: Emotionally prepare patients and families for changes in their lives (Level IV)

Preparing the patient and family for the transition means taking the necessary steps and time to involve them. Although the process may seem elementary, it is more complex than it first appears. Nurses and other clinical professionals know intuitively that patients' needs will be addressed in a long-term care or other skilled nursing environment, but the patient and family don't necessarily know this. Reassure patients that they will be cared for and will receive help doing whatever they need to do. Let them know that they will not be ignored.

Preparing patients also means monitoring and being aware of patients' and families' emotional experiences. Go beyond the obvious signs of emotional crisis and identify the patients and families quietly struggling with their emotions. Work to match patients and families with appropriate psychosocial interventions to head off the emotional problems of anxiety, depression, and stress. Several approaches hold universal potential:

- Screen for patients at high risk of needing psychiatric counseling.

- Psychologically prepare elective-surgery patients as early as possible. An educational video sent to the patient's home in the week prior to admission reduces anxiety and improves coping ability.

- Integrate relaxation techniques into practices and procedures. Teaching the patient a relaxation technique before providing patient education can improve medication compliance and knowledge retention and can potentially reduce the length of stay.

Words that work

Alleviating stress

Patients tend to experience the greatest stress, fear, and anxiety immediately before surgery, tests, and other procedures.

Therefore, prior to a test or procedure (e.g., administering anesthesia, inserting an IV, inserting a catheter, delivering patient education), ask patients the following:

- *How are you feeling?*
- *How do you feel about this?*
- *Do you feel tense?*

Because most patients will reply with the socially desirable response (i.e., "Okay"), directly ask all patients questions that will help form a bond of trust:

- *I want to help you relax. Will you try a breathing exercise with me?*
- *Would you like to try a technique that always helps me relax?*

Stretching exercises, breathing exercises, meditation, and progressive muscle relaxation are all techniques that you can teach patients.

Best practice: Evaluate the emotional experience of processes, eliminate stressors, and maximize positive emotions (Level IV)

Evaluating the emotional experience of processes that may stress a patient brings a new perspective to bear on quality. Events that appear devoid of emotion to staff can be anxiety-inducing for patients. Therefore, systematically evaluate every point along the myriad series of events from before admission through postdischarge. Determine what can be done to prevent or reduce anxiety (and other negative emotions).

2. Poor first impressions of the sub-acute or home healthcare experience immediately postdischarge

Patients' first impressions of the healthcare services you arranged are their final impressions of your facility and staff. By arranging for or recommending a health service, you stand behind the quality of that service. To use a marketing term, this is called "co-mingling of brands." In the minds of customers, good or bad experiences with one organization will affect their opinion of both that organization and the affiliated organization.

It's not enough to simply identify that a patient will need home healthcare and provide a list of agencies from which they can randomly choose. Instead, do everything possible to set up the agency for success. Recognize and take responsibility for the relationship with these organizations, and use your leadership role to facilitate the transition to your patients' benefit.

Best practice: Cross-organizational or cross-departmental collaborative service quality improvement (Level IV)

Best-performing organizations proactively collaborate across organizations or departments, taking an active and vested interest in the quality of service across the care continuum. This means reaching out beyond your area or organization to collaborate, share, and improve together:

- Share the process flow charts you create for mapping the discharge process into a nursing home or home health agency (see the introduction for more information.) Better yet, if you're just starting, work on these diagrams together.

- Have monthly process review meetings with the admissions/intake staff of nursing homes and/or home health agencies to make certain the process is going smoothly and identify and take action on any outstanding issues that create roadblocks to a smooth transition.

- Share proven practices that you've implemented. If you have service standards, trainings, or reward and recognition programs that have been effective—why not share them? Think of all the similar activities that you and your extended care colleagues engage in and consider working together in the development or improvement of these activities.

Making it work

Patient visits

At Mills Peninsula Extended Care in Burlingame, CA, the administrator visits all patients within one or two days of admission (but typically on the same day). The administrator shares information about the facility and provides a facility manual that contains contact information and phone numbers. The activities coordinator also visits with patients personally on the day of admission to familiarize them with the amenities that the facility offers and proactively sign them up for activities.

Goal records

At Johnson City (TN) Medical Center and the James H. & Cecile C. Quilen Rehabilitation Hospital, also in Johnson City, therapy staff developed "Goal Records" that they complete during the session to mark patients' progress. Patients receive a copy of the goal record to take back to their rooms. The sheets ensure that patients are included in their daily goal setting, can see their progress, and can show their family their progress.

Small details can make a big difference in a patient's stay. Try one or more of the following:

- **Nurse-to-nurse calls:** Have the patient's nurse call the nurse at the nursing home, home healthcare agency, or rehab hospital and talk to the patient's new nurse. In less than five minutes, the nurses can confirm the patient's medical history (which should already be in hand) and informally discuss aspects of the patient's personal situation critical to effective interpersonal relationships and communication. After the phone call, tell the patient or family about the conversation. Most patients and family members will find it comforting to hear that you called to check up and make sure everything was ready.

- **Provide direct contact information:** Postacute health services often will only receive the general phone number for the unit where the patient stayed. Typically, this is not helpful because most nurses on a unit will be unfamiliar with the case—only the nurse who provided the majority of the care will know exactly what is going on. No one should have to wait for potentially critical information because there is a lapse in communication or accessibility. Therefore, when you make the nurse-to-nurse call, give the future nurse a direct line where you can be reached to answer questions and provide information.

- **Emphasize teamwork and collaboration by using shared language:** Consider the difference between *my patients* or *I have a patient* and *our patient* or *we have a patient*. Our words make a difference. They can reinforce the shared collaboration or they can create a wall between provider organizations or departments.

Making it work

Changing patient perceptions

In its journey from the 6th to the 71st percentile, Ingalls Hospital in Harvey, IL, worked with its affiliated Inpatient Rehabilitation Service to improve its services and care processes. Improvements in the rehabilitation unit that affected inpatient perceptions included the following:

- Upon arriving on the unit, nursing assistants use a scripted greeting that highlights what the patient can expect. The patient receives an informational packet, a welcome gift containing an assortment of convenience items, and an invitation to a patient/family orientation class.

- Hourly rounds reduce the number of call lights. RNs assess and treat pain on an ongoing basis.

- Physical, occupational, recreational, and speech therapy goal sheets identifying the patient's rehabilitation goals are posted in the patient's room. Staff and family are encouraged to help the patient reach these goals.

- The patient and a guest are invited to a special dinner to celebrate their upcoming discharge.

- The patient's "graduation" from the program is celebrated with team members through songs of encouragement, applause, and a certificate.

- On discharge day, the nursing team presents the patient with an angel pin and a bookmark and personally thanks the patient for choosing Ingalls Center for Rehabilitative Medicine.

- An attempt is made to contact all patients within 10 days after discharge. Patient input is tracked and shared with the patient satisfaction team.

     Patient Satisfaction and the Discharge Process

3. The patient/family cannot afford the home healthcare arrangements

The number of uninsured patients continues to grow, making solid inroads into the middle income brackets. Further, many predict that the next five years will see an explosion of high-deductible consumer-directed health plans, where patients pay up to the first $10,000 of their care. Regardless of what the future may hold, however, healthcare affordability is a problem. Postdischarge health services, including home healthcare arrangements, pharmaceuticals, medical equipment, or other items that would optimize recovery, may be sacrificed.

Best practice: Check for financial obstacles and provide financial counseling (Level IV)

Patients and their families may be facing the loss of their primary income, the added responsibility of caregiving, and massive hospital bills. They may be terrified of going bankrupt from paying such bills. Financial counseling services not only improve patient satisfaction but are also good for the healthcare organization's bottom line.

Making it work

There are several ways in which you can help patients with their financial needs:

- **Make financial counseling standard for self-pay patients:** Self-pay patients are more likely to be in need of financial counseling. A preliminary assessment may be all that is needed.

- **Obtain precise pricing information or the best estimates possible:** Get prices to patients and families up front (even at preadmission for elective surgeries) to enable good financial planning. Patients not only want to know prices, they also want the ability to shop around. When structuring your process for arranging home healthcare services, don't think about how you've done things in the past. Instead, think in the mindset of insurance and mortgage companies: Provide quotes from several companies for comparison within seconds.

- **Couple with patient liaison/advocate activities, customer service training for counselors and other staff, and scripting:** Patient liaisons, patient advocates, social workers, discharge planners, or other hospital staff dedicated to cultivating the relationship with patients are in a good position to identify financially at-risk patients early in their stay. They can use their position working on behalf of the patient to get to know the patient's

---

Making it work (cont.)

situation on these sensitive issues. Staff involved in financial counseling should all be rigorously trained in communication and customer service skills. Scripts such as the following are appropriate for consistency and to ensure that sensitive questions are asked with the tact and grace necessary to obtain a response:

- *This is a new addition to your monthly expenses, so we always check with our patients just to make sure that the*

medications can be purchased today to get you started right away. But you will be taking this for several months, maybe longer, so how will this new expense work out for you financially?
- *We've talked about your postdischarge plan and the challenges you'll be facing. For many patients, another hurdle is just fitting the costs for these medications and equipment into their budget. It can squeeze things a bit. (Wait for an answer.)*

---

4. Family members are unable to cope with the postdischarge caregiving or support needs

For many, family members are unpaid home health aides. It's a rare situation when a family member is not providing care activities in addition to sustaining the home environment by assuming most activities of daily living. Often, the strongest predictor of whether a patient maintains adherence to therapies, medications, or other postdischarge regimens is the support (or lack thereof) given by the closest family member. Therefore, engaging family members is good for the patient and the facility—and, in the long-run, family members may be future customers.

Best practice: Family meetings (Level III)

Family meetings are often an effective way to

simultaneously communicate much needed information quickly while gathering the family and doctor(s), including specialists, nurses, and discharge planners/social workers. They can help prepare a patient for his or her future, whether it be home care, long-term care, or palliative care.

Indeed, patient experiences postdischarge are far better when a family meeting occurs with all members of the care team. Contradicting information is clarified, and often specialists will be able to see each other face to face for the first time to come to a consensus on any differences in prognosis or other assessments. Most important, it puts everyone on the same page—the patient's page—regarding goals of care. The patient learns most definitively what is going on, and everyone else learns what is important to the

 Patient Satisfaction and the Discharge Process

patient. Proven practices for increasing the use of family meetings include the following:

- Hardwire a family meeting as a requirement along certain clinical pathways.

- Hold substantial training that gives clinicians and staff the opportunity to see how a family meeting is run, and practice running one.

- Have attendings teach residents how to conduct these meetings. Monitor this for consistency.

- Put together a toolkit or best practice guideline document that outlines the fundamentals of a family meeting.

Best practice: In-depth caregiver and family assessment and education (Level II)

Caregivers need information long before a family meeting is called. They need to understand the illness, what to expect as the illness lessens or progresses, special diets or health strategies that might benefit the patient, and education on fundamentals such as caring techniques, meal preparation tips, symptoms (including which ones should or should not warrant professional medical attention), pain management techniques (including non-pharmacologic techniques), community resources, and support groups. Particularly in cases of extended home recuperation, the caregiver could benefit substantially from learning coping, time management, stress

reduction, and personal health maintenance skills. Beyond the realm of skills and caring, the family's emotional readiness also should be considered a component of assessment and education. Carrying out such an in-depth assessment often encourages substantial family involvement and input.

Making it work

Intake form

At Vanderbilt Children's Hospital in Nashville, TN, the Family Resource Center staff welcome new families using an intake form that assesses their information needs and learning style. Staff then assemble personalized packets of information on topics of interest to the family, including their child's disease(s), available financial support, educational programs, and community resources.

The resource center has also created an informational notebook for families of hematology and oncology patients. Developed by a team of physicians, nurses, and social workers, the notebook features information about the child's specific illness and uses color-coded pages to help families prioritize their reading. Families also participate in targeted educational programs developed by the center in response to requests from the hospital's family support groups.

Hospital causes

1. The hospital failed to identify and make arrangements for activities of daily living

Activities of daily living (ADLs) typically include six undertakings that comprise our abilities to care for ourselves: bathing, dressing, transferring, using the toilet, eating, and walking. The majority of patients discharged from your facility will have limitations at some level that will hinder their ability to act as they did before their stay. It is up to your facility to ensure that all ADLs are assessed and documented.

Best practice: Assess all patients for their ability to cope at home (Level III)

Many patients, especially the elderly and those who score low on ADL assessments, will need a fuller assessment during discharge planning. For many acute care facilities, this type of preliminary assessment has become standard practice. Nevertheless, consider *how* this assessment is completed. Some will approach it as yet more paperwork and simply seek to complete the form as quickly as possible based on their own judgments. Best-performing facilities in patient satisfaction with discharge will use the assessment as a tool to *interact with the patient,* briefly discussing each point with patients and families, soliciting their perspective, and using the assessment as a springboard to review what they will need in order to copy postdischarge.

Progressive hospitals don't stop at assessing ADLs. Hard-wired assessments of the instrumental activities of daily living (IADL) are the next step. IADLs are six everyday jobs that determine our capacity for successfully living on our own in the community:

- Light housework
- Making meals
- Managing medications
- Shopping for groceries, clothes, and medications
- Using a telephone
- Managing finances

Often IADLs will fly under the radar of healthcare professionals and even patients themselves. We typically take these activities for granted, so health changes that limit our ability to execute previously easy, mundane activities can be overlooked. Part of preparing patients for a successful transition home is reviewing these activities during discharge planning with patients and family members.

The final step in ensuring that appropriate arrangements have been made for ADLs and IADLs is to include a review of these activities in your follow-up care procedures. In postdischarge phone calls, ask patients how they are managing each of the ADLs and IADLs. In doing so, you not only ensure the patient's successful, safe, and satisfactory transition, but you also demonstrate the depth with which your organization cares about his or her well-being.

 Patient Satisfaction and the Discharge Process

2. Failure to develop a long-term relationship with the patient and family

If your last communication with patients takes place as they leave your facility, don't expect high marks on this leg of the survey. As patients and caregivers begin the next part of the healing process, any hurt and frustration can easily be turned toward your facility. By developing a relationship with patients that goes beyond their stay, you offer better, more comprehensive healthcare—and your patients will notice.

Best practice: Postdischarge phone calls (Level I)

If you only implement one best practice from this book, make it this one. No other intervention has such a consistent and decidedly positive effect on so many outcomes. The simple act of calling every patient after they've left the hospital is a true loyalty builder and market differentiator. It is an opportunity to express gratitude and empathy to the patient. Few other services in any industry will call you to personally ask about your experience. Benefits include improved

- patient satisfaction
- response rates to patient satisfaction surveys
- patient compliance with medication regimens, therapies, and appointments
- medication safety
- understanding of your patients' perception of service
- clinical outcomes

Making it work

Cultivating an ongoing, long-term relationship

After discharge from Floyd Medical Center in Rome, GA, a staff member calls the patient to check on the transition to home, and an additional follow-up is conducted in another three months. Staff encourage patients to attend one of several support groups for continued access to assistance.

Following are answers to common questions facilities ask as they embark on postdischarge phone calls:

- *Who makes the calls?*
    - Nurses don't need to make the calls. The caller simply needs access to a nurse if questions arise.

- *Do you call* **all** *patients?*
    - Call as many patients as possible.

- *Do you speak only to the patient?*
    - Speak only to the patient unless he or she has already designated another individual.

- *How many attempts do you make?*
    - Try twice. Vary the time of day you call. Some patients, typically the elderly, will be home during the day.

Others, typically younger patients, may be at work during the day, so evenings may be the best time to call.

- *Do you leave a message?*
  - Do not leave a message per compliance with the Health Insurance Portability and Accountability Act of 1996.
  - If you do leave a message, make sure it is ambiguous, with no names or specifics regarding procedures.

See Appendix E for more tips on making phone calls and sample scripts to use.

Best practice: Express to patients the importance of filling out the survey (Level IV)

Today, our society responds less and less to telephone or mailed surveys unless we *know that they make a difference*. Integrating practices that improve response rates into your follow-up procedures will increase the number of responses, smooth out natural variation, and eliminate huge swings in your scores or percentile rankings. From a statistical perspective, this provides improved quality control. From the perspective of your staff and executive management, predictability in scores—knowing that if satisfaction rises or falls it definitely has a cause—boosts both employee morale and executive buy-in, respectively.

Best practice: Recommend hospital, health system, or community resources (Level IV)

Whatever your official role—discharge planner, social worker, nurse, or other provider—if you're actively working with the patient, consider the patient's long-term health needs. Don't be trapped by considering only what they need to recover or what your facility can offer. It doesn't matter who provides it; if a resource you recommended effectively meets their needs, they will associate that experience with you. Keep a file of healthcare and wellness resources for staff members to refer to in regular patient contact. Include a comprehensive list along with ancillary information, such as brochures and business cards for support groups, social clubs, therapeutic masseuses, illness-specific groups, AA or Al-Anon, Weight Watchers, and many other organizations. Patients and family members will trust your recommendations for information sources, health promotion, social activity, and other resources.

Making it work

Your opinion counts

Brown County General Hospital (BCGH) in Georgetown, OH, designed numerous practices to improve response rates directly into the discharge process. BCGH decided the first thing patients needed to know was that their experience was important and launched a "Your Opinion Counts" theme. During the hospital stay, a flyer in each patient's room reminds patients to complete the survey. Posters publicizing the "Your Opinion Counts" message hang in the nursing units, in patient waiting areas, and by timekeepers for staff.

Upon discharge, each patient receives a pen with the message "Your Opinion Counts." The staff member providing the discharge instructions tells the patient that a survey will be mailed and asks that it be filled out, whether the ratings were good or bad. A sticker is placed on the patient's copy of the discharge instructions as an additional reminder.

To take the process a step further, the communications/celebration team initiated follow-up phone calls to patients after discharge. Mail-back response rates climbed to 20% during the first quarter of implementation and jumped to 35% during the second quarter. As a test to determine the effectiveness of the follow-up, calls were suspended for one quarter—and response rates dropped to 22%. The team immediately reinstated the follow-up calls and formed a separate team to handle them. Response rates increased to 39% and 45% during the first two quarters after reinstatement.

Conclusion

The following true story underscores the fact that even the slightest misunderstanding in instruction has potentially disastrous consequences. At discharge, the patient was attentive and listening to the instructions on the medication regimen. She had three family members with her who were also attentive and writing down the instructions given by the doctor and nurse. They even took the extra step of drawing up a medication schedule that specified times during the day for different medicines based on the instructions on the bottles. The problem was that those instructions were followed literally. Ambien was prescribed, and the instructions stated to take every four hours—but failed to mentioned the all-important words: *as needed for sleep.* This resulted in a patient sleeping almost constantly for the first three days after she arrived home. The concerned family called a neurologist friend, and he immediately set things right by advising that Ambien should only be taken as needed when one has trouble falling asleep.

Perhaps the doctor and nurse assumed that everyone should know that Ambien is only to be taken as needed. Perhaps it just wasn't caught in the conversation. Regardless, it's important to remember that even with engaged, interested, and devoted patients and family members, a little lack of effective communication can have large consequences.

Consider what could have helped in this situation and what could have been done differently. Many of the best practices reviewed in this chapter (and this book) could have helped. A follow-up phone call within 48 hours of discharge would likely have picked up the issue. Testing for understanding by asking patients or family members to repeat back their understanding of the instructions also could have helped, along with reviewing the medication schedule in the comprehensive discharge planning session.

The remainder of the best practices discussed in this chapter focused on preparing patients to change their lives—to adapt to the new realities of their condition. Patients and families will need to adapt—both at the hospital and at home, emotionally, financially, in their daily living routine, and in their family dynamic. Family meetings, caregiver assessments, financial counseling, and addressing emotional needs are all practices targeting these fundamental facts of leaving the hospital that require additional work beyond the typical discharge to facilitate the transition.

Best practices for focused improvement

Learning objectives

By the end of this chapter, you should be able to

- explain the steps in the PDCA cycle

- summarize the role a concierge service can play in the discharge process

- describe tactics used by several top performing hospitals to organize, manage, and lead high achievement in patient satisfaction

- list two ways in which volunteers can help maintain/promote patient satisfaction

- understand the organizational and management implications for implementing best practices and creating a world-class discharge process

Many hospitals handle the same issues in different ways and still experience positive outcomes. The first half of this chapter looks at different best practices in areas such as how the survey information makes its way from the page to the plan, staff education and investment, the patient's physical surroundings, and use of volunteers. The second half of this chapter provides a real-life example of what it takes to put a plan in place. We will follow a yearlong process to get one plan—a concierge system—up and running at one facility.

Acting on the survey information

The best way to understand how to keep patients happy is to read the results of the patient satisfaction survey. But with the potential for receiving thousands of them each year, the decision of **who** will read the surveys is a big question for a busy facility. Beyond reading the results, using the data to make positive changes can feel like a task too large to tackle. Facilities need to choose a method that works best for their organization to get that

information off the page and into the plan for success.

The Services Excellence Committee

The director of patient services at Greenwich (CT) Hospital reads every survey (approximately 3,000 per year) and divides comments into categories of positive and negative. Then a senior-level management group, consisting of 37 individuals (including several vice presidents, all department directors, and every clinical manager) and chaired by the president/CEO and director of patient services, meets weekly for one hour. The committee reviews a report generated from every complaint received (including surveys marked with a score of 3 or lower for the past week). This report is sometimes 75 pages long, and managers are queried if the same problem/area repeatedly appears from one week to the next. This system creates a public structure of accountability. If a negative patient satisfaction issue arises, the meeting provides a forum to air it in a transparent and timely fashion. It does not become stale waiting until the monthly or quarterly report.

Patient Satisfaction and the Discharge Process

Making it work

Comment extraction

At Greenwich Hospital, Greenwich, CT positive survey comments that name a hospital employee are copied. The president/CEO signs a personalized thank you card that has the positive comment printed inside, and the card is sent to the employee. Surveys with perfect scores are copied and sent to the manager with a congratulations message. These actions emphasize to staff that doing a great job really counts.

Patient relations department

At Centra Health System in Lynchburg, VA, each of the two hospitals have two nurses who work within the marketing department. This small sub-department functions as a hotline and resource for all units to draw upon to meet any patient request (e.g., arranging for in-hospital wedding and birthday celebrations for patients, obtaining CD players and specific music at patients' requests). In addition, these nurses read every patient satisfaction survey. They log complaints into a database and distribute comment reports to the appropriate units for future action.

Creating a dynamic staff

The best plans and scripts will do nothing to raise discharge satisfaction levels if it is clear to your patients that staff lack the social and medical skills necessary to help them to heal. Patients will have questions, and staff must be able to respond—either with the clinical information they need or with a customer-focused answer that puts patients at ease until a proper answer can be delivered.

Customer service training

Centra Health employed a consultant to develop a customer service training program for all associates. More than 20 hours of employee training each year is devoted to customer service/patient satisfaction, and the massive initial training has transformed into a curriculum for all new associates.

Lexington Medical Center (LMC) in West Columbia, SC, also conducts customer service training. Each employee is cross-trained and participates in more than 300 hours of training. This education has caused a massive culture change and improved patient satisfaction. The change efforts were buoyed by simultaneous initiatives that reinforce the importance of service in culture and deed:

- Employee satisfaction is measured regularly, and improvements are made based on the results.

- A patient satisfaction incentive/bonus program was created for all staff. The annual amount has varied between $100 and 2% of an employee's salary.

Making it work

Service with a Passion

LMC's "Service with a Passion" program emphasizes basic customer service philosophy, establishes expectations, and teaches service recovery. To drive home the message that every employee's actions affect the patient's experience in the cycle of service, all staff in the organization (2,700) were required to participate in the classes. Each participant learned how to address customer concerns and thank patients for sharing their concerns with a G.I.F.T.: Give a sincere apology; Inform the patient of how you will address their concerns; Fix the problem, follow through, and follow up; and Thank the patient for bringing the issue to your attention with a gift bag. The radiology department took this initiative to heart and gave the most G.I.F.T. bags for the year in order to recover from many long wait-time situations.

To emphasize the importance of customer service, LMC created an educational program dubbed "Service with a Passion."

Organizational learning

Each case manager at Metropolitan Hospital in Grand Rapids, MI, has a specialty diagnosis for which he or she assumes responsibility. They keep up-to-date on the latest advancements through literature, education, etc., and they communicate this knowledge to other staff members as needed and serve as an expert resource for nurses and doctors.

Making it work

Maintaining an edge

Metropolitan Hospital provides membership for all case managers in the Case Management Society of America (*www.cmsa.org*) as well as funds for meeting attendance and continuing education. Nurses are active in the society and have readily adopted its philosophy of empowering patients with information, education, and choices. To ensure good work, case managers perform monthly peer review on each others' charts. Information gathered through this process is put into a graphical chart form to show, as a group, the areas that need more focus.

Patient Satisfaction and the Discharge Process

Measuring up in the waiting room

It's easy to focus so much on revamping the verbal interaction with patients and caregivers that an organization can lose sight of the other ways in which it can serve its customers. Small changes in the physical surroundings can relax patients and help caregivers to stay calm through a potentially long process.

Patient room and waiting room décor

Centra Health System gave its pediatrics unit a facelift that brightened the area, enlarged the rooms, set up private rooms, and made the unit more child- and family-friendly. The hospital installed gliding rockers in patient rooms to improve comfort and added scenic pictures for a more pleasant atmosphere. Centra installed VCRs in each of its pediatric rooms, and area businesses donated children's videos.

The waiting areas at Centra contain

- diversions such as puzzles, magazines, word searches, and mind-bogglers in addition to television.

- internal privacy phones located in the waiting area link to surgical units for staff/ physicians to call out for updates to families. An additional public phone is also available for making outside calls.

- suggestion boxes for patient and family comments.

LMC took a unique approach and made the main waiting room smaller rather than larger. As soon as patients are registered, they are taken to a sub-waiting room for the specific area in which they will receive their test. They are grouped with patients receiving similar tests, so the wait times are comparable. Cameras in the waiting rooms allow technicians and assistants to monitor patients and how long they have been waiting. This system prompts them to communicate any delays.

Getting the most out of volunteers

Volunteers in your facility might be good candidates for observing and listening to patients' emotional and/or technical needs while the staff are bustling about. Motivate and empower them by including them in important tasks that lend to patient satisfaction.

The volunteers at Centra Health Systems are well-trained, articulate, and dedicated to the hospital. They are selected carefully and attend training that lasts a little more than a week. They provide the following support:

- **Rounding.** Volunteers visit patients every day. They ask a standard set of questions.

- **Service recovery.** In the event that they encounter an upset customer, volunteers have the same access to service recovery resources as staff do (i.e., $3 gift shop vouchers, $5 meal vouchers, and $15 gift shop vouchers). Patient relations is very explicit with the volunteers on the expectations and opportunities that accompany their position.

- **"Teddy."** Volunteers make small care bears, which nurses date and sign for pediatric patients upon discharge.

- **Courtesy refreshment cart.** The plant engineering department built a mobile cart, which volunteers roll around hourly to offer coffee, muffins, and fruit to families waiting.

Putting a plan in place: A view into one year

The Boston-based Harvard Community Health Plan and Brigham and Women's Hospital (a 700-bed teaching hospital affiliated with the Harvard Medical School) have collaborated on patient care for the past 20 years. Since 1986, the hospital has been the major site of secondary and tertiary care for the majority of patients in the HMO's Health Centers Division. The HMO maintains administrative offices at the hospital and works closely with the hospital's clinical and administrative staff on quality improvement (QI) and utilization management.[1]

The challenge

Data collected in spring 1994 from Brigham and Women's Hospital's Patient Satisfaction Survey (PSS), which included responses from the HMO's members, revealed that there was less satisfaction with hospital discharge planning than with other elements of care. For example, whereas 96% (640 of 667) of patients rated the overall care at the hospital as excellent or very good, only 73% (496) rated the hospital discharge planning process as such. Seeking to improve the satisfaction of its members, the HMO creatively challenged the hospital to improve patients' ratings of discharge planning: It offered a financial incentive in exchange for a measurable, time-specified performance standard met within a 12-month period.

The explicit goal, as established by senior administration from the hospital and HMO, challenged the team to improve discharge satisfaction of adult medical patients on one patient unit. It was to increase from a baseline of 73% of patients rating discharge planning as excellent or very good to 81% in 12 months.

The hospital and HMO had a history of collaborating to improve such processes as wait times in the emergency department and operating rooms and time for tests to be reported. However, establishing a goal with patient satisfaction as a measure of improvement was new; no empiric information was found in the literature to guide the extent of improvement to be expected in 12 months. Thus, the hospital and HMO agreed on a goal that appeared reasonable but for which there were no examples of best practice improvement.

When this challenge was presented, the hospital's discharge planning process for patients was complex and involved participation from several departments (e.g., nursing, social work, escort, pharmacy, valet, and medicine) that were not administratively linked. The process was not standardized, and no department oversaw discharge coordination and efficiency. Although the hospital employed case managers for specific patient groups, case managers' responsibility in the discharge planning process focused more on clinical issues, such as arranging appropriate discharge placement or home services for patients, than on the logistic issues and events associated with a patient's departure from the hospital (e.g., discharge instructions reviewed with the patient in a timely manner, wheelchair and cart [if needed] arrives within an acceptable amount of time after discharge, medications explained in a way the patient can understand, etc.).

In response to the HMO's challenge, senior administrators from the HMO and the hospital created an interdisciplinary team of members from both organizations to design and implement strategies to meet the performance standard. The hospital's Department of Quality Measurement and Improvement fully supported this team because it was a win-win situation for both orga-

nizations: The HMO could better address the needs and expectations of its members, and the hospital would be more able to meet the needs and expectations of two sets of customers—its patients and the HMO.

Creating the team
Brigham and Women's first move toward quality improvement (QI) was to create an interdisciplinary team. The hospital followed three key guidelines to successful teams in organizations:

- Choose no more than six to eight carefully elected individuals

- State a common and clearly stated purpose and goal

- Set clear team leadership

Eight individuals were selected for the team on the basis of their knowledge, skills, and involvement in the discharge process of medical patients. They represented a wide range of hospital functions and departments:

Hospital
- Two medical staff nurses

- One nurse manager from a general medicine patient unit

- One general medicine resident

- One nurse researcher/director of quality measurement

HMO

- One nurse case manager
- Two internal medicine physicians

The hospital's nurse and one of the HMO physicians shared leadership responsibility for the team. The hospital's nurse researcher, who had joint responsibility in the Departments of Nursing and Quality Measurement and Improvement, oversaw and coordinated the team's work. Two research assistants from the hospital's Departments of Quality Measurement and Improvement and Nursing Research were available to the team for selected projects, such as reviewing literature, collecting data, and implementing short-term improvement strategies.

Brigham and Women's second move was to identify a process by which they would reach their QI goal. The team chose to follow the Plan-Do-Check-Act (PDCA) cycle. This method calls for understanding the process, including its problems and root causes, before attempting improvement strategies. Once the process is clearly understood, the design of PDCA can be implemented.

To better understand the discharge planning process and its associated problems, the team designed and deployed the following three-part process:

- Collect patient feedback

- Design a flowchart of the discharge planning process

- Synthesize flow chart and patient feedback data

Patient feedback

Patient feedback information was derived from two sources: the patient satisfaction survey (PSS) and telephone interviews with patients who were recently discharged from the hospital.

On the PSS, 73% rated the discharge process with the top two ratings. However, although this single-item rating provided the baseline metric for the team's goal, it provided no detail about the specific issues and problems associated with discharge planning.

A second source of patient feedback information was provided via telephone interviews with a randomly selected 17% of patients, or 20 of the 85 patients discharged from a medical patient unit during the prior week. During the 15- to 30-minute interviews, trained research assistants first asked patients to describe the day of discharge and then followed up with specific questions about their discharge. Interviews were recorded and transcribed, and common themes for improvement were noted. Although most comments were favorable, the following problematic themes were noted:

- The amount of time patients waited for the escort to bring them to the lobby for their discharge

- The amount of time patients waited for their discharge medications at their payers' pharmacies

- Patients' surprise and frustration with their primary care physicians' lack of awareness about their recent hospitalization

- Patients' perceptions of a lack of coordination among staff about discharge decisions and a general lack of knowledge among staff regarding when discharges were scheduled to occur

Flow charting information

The team also gathered information about discharge planning by creating flow charts of the process. The flow charts pointed out the lack of standardization and coordination in the discharge planning process and excessive wait times for patients. However, it also noted specific problem areas, such as the following:

- How the decision about discharge was communicated among the team

- Who provides the patient with discharge information

- The time elapsed from when the patient or nurse is informed of discharge to when the discharge order is actually written by the physician

- The time it takes an escort to arrive on the unit after being called to discharge a patient

- The time patients wait for their medication prescriptions to be filled at their payers' pharmacies

- The irregularity with which follow-up appointments are scheduled for patients after discharge

Synthesis of patient feedback and flow-charting information

Using the information collected through patient feedback and flow charts, the team generated the following list of discharge planning–related problems at Brigham and Women's:

- Patients and staff were not clear about who was responsible for making decisions about discharge and follow-up care

- Patients and staff had unrealistic expectations of the inpatient experience, which is one small episode on the care continuum (which may include experiences in the emergency department, various lab and testing units, physician office visits, etc.)

- Communication between patients' care providers, especially those responsible for hospital care and postdischarge/ambulatory care, was poor or inconsistent

- Discharge systems were inefficient and uncoordinated

- Postdischarge follow-up with patients was erratic. There was no clear signal of a successful hand-off between the hospital and

sub-acute providers (i.e., primary care provider, skilled nursing facility, etc.)

Improvement Cycle 1

Armed with the knowledge gained about the discharge planning process and its problems, the team went to work designing a PDCA cycle. The team ultimately decided to perform two cycles, using the second cycle as an opportunity to incorporate any findings from Cycle 1. A full depiction of Cycle 1 appears in Figure 6.1.

 6.1 FIGURE

PDCA for Cycle 1

Step	Team actions
Plan	• Created two sequential improvement cycles over nine months • Established two objectives for Cycle 1: 　- Designed an improvement strategy for discharge planning that was easy to deploy and evaluate in a four-month window 　- Decided to lessons learned in Cycle 1 to design a better Cycle 2
Do	Designed a temporary discharge concierge service of two research assistants to keep patients informed of status
Check	Patient satisfaction surveys sent to patients who received the concierge services were compared against those from patients who did not receive concierge services
Act	Drew on the results of Cycle 1 and designed a subsequent set of improvement strategies

Patient Satisfaction and the Discharge Process

Concierge service

The primary focus of Cycle 1 was to initiate a concierge service to help with discharge. The two research assistants chosen for this role provided the following services:

- Coordinated a delay-free discharge process

- Relayed information to patients and families about the status of the discharge (e.g., when their discharge order was written, when their discharge medications were ready, and when discharge prescriptions were faxed to the payer's pharmacy)

- Organized delay-free transportation for patients to the hospital lobby

The service, it was decided, would be available to a subset of patients discharged from one medical floor. The subset included patients who were discharged during the month of March, Monday through Friday, 8 a.m. to 6 p.m. However, patients who were discharged to a nursing home or rehabilitation facility or who were discharged by ambulance were ineligible to receive the concierge service.

The findings of Cycle 1

Patients who received the discharge concierge services rated the process higher than patients who did not receive the service. Specifically, 83% of patients in the intervention group gave the highest two ratings while only 63% of patients in the

control group gave the highest two ratings (see Figure 6.2).

Therefore, the team drew on the results of Cycle 1 and the discharge problems generated during the problem identification process to design the second set of improvement strategies.

As mentioned earlier, the discharge concierge intervention addressed only one problem associated with discharge: the delays and wait time related to dispensing medications and escorting patients to the lobby for discharge. Strategies to address the remaining problems would be introduced during the next four-month period.

Improvement Cycle 2

Once the results of Cycle 1 were obtained, preparation began for implementation of Cycle 2. There were four areas of concern targeted in Cycle 2 as a result of the Cycle 1 evaluation:

1. Patients and staff were not clear about who was responsible for making decisions about discharge and follow-up care.

2. Patients and staff had unrealistic expectations of hospitalization within the context of the care continuum.

3. Discharge systems were inefficient and uncoordinated.

4. Communication between patients' care providers, especially between those responsible for hospital care and post-discharge/ambulatory care, was poor or inconsistent.

Again, the team comprised of 4-6 subgroups from within the organization, worked on the PDCA cycle and Figure 6.2 below outlines the findings. Two people from the original Cycle 1 took ownership for these subgroups and their work.

6.2 FIGURE

PCDA for Cycle 2

Step	Team actions
Plan	
Do	***Implement improvement strategies (Cycle 2).*** The multidimensional improvement strategies were implemented during September 1995 for all HMO patients who were discharged home via care on Mondays through Fridays, from 8 AM to 6 PM (N=105).
Check	***Evaluate the improvement strategies (Cycle 2).*** Of the 40 patient satisfaction surveys (40 of 105) that were returned by HMO patients, 18 patients received the discharge services and 24 did not. (See Figure 6.3)
Act	***Determine next steps (Cycle 2).*** Using the results from two improvement cycles to improve patients' satisfaction with discharge, the team presented a set of recommendations and associated costs to the hospital and HMO. The strategies implemented in both improvement cycles were conducted on one patient unit; implications of hospital-wide implementation will require thoughtful examination.

Cycle 2 began in June 1995, and included 105 patients who were discharged Monday through Friday between 8 a.m. and 6 p.m. The sample group only included patients who were discharged to their homes, and not those that died or were discharged to non-acute care facilities.

The Findings of Cycle 2

There were a total of 40 responses out of 105 mailed surveys (a response rate of 42%). Of the 40 respondents, only 18 of them actually received the discharge concierge services and 24 did not (referred to as the "control group"). As seen in Figure 6.3, 83% rated the discharge services as

Patient Satisfaction and the Discharge Process

excellent or very good (those that received the concierge-type of discharge services outlined in Cycle 1), as compared with 73% rating their experience with discharge as being very good or excellent without the concierge services. There was an increase of 10% (for those that rated their discharge experience very good or excellent, from 73% to 83%) if they received the concierge discharge services. This let the team know not only that the concierge idea was instrumental in increasing the satisfaction scores for the discharge section on the survey, but also allowed them to see how much of an impact it has on the overall score.

6.3 FIGURE

Payers' patient satisfaction with discharge planning: Control and intervention groups during Cycle 2

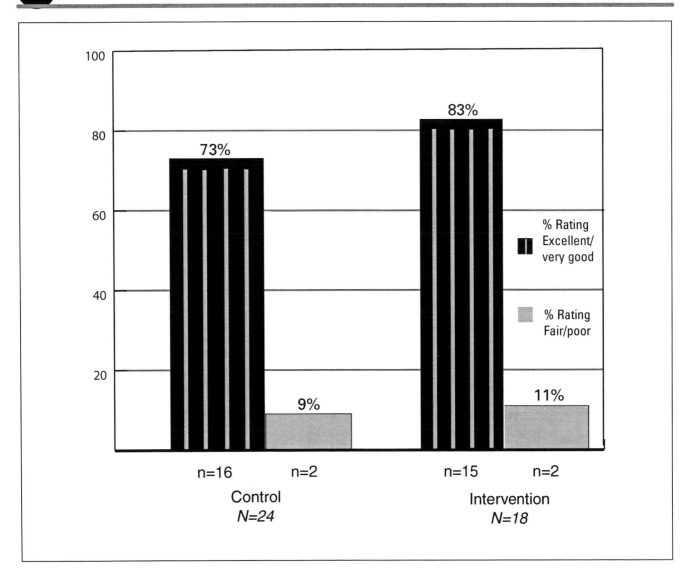

The results provided the hospital and HMO information that allowed them to see the relationship between managed care, expectations of staff and patients regarding discharge, how the continuum of care relates to those involved with it and a better handle of the effects that slow processes and systems have on the discharge process and the associated levels of patient satisfaction.

While the small patient sample meant that a statistical analysis could not be done, Cycle 2 still provided insight into the overall processes and clinical systems that support the discharge process. It also served as a valuable experience for those involved on the hospital side.

Conclusion

A team's experience on one patient unit has offered the hospital and the HMO a great deal of information about the discharge planning process, associated problems, opportunities for improvement, and successful improvement strategies that ensure service quality. The knowledge gained through this incremental improvement work has provided the hospital and HMO with substantive information from which to consider hospitalwide implementation.

The improvement cycle methodology provided the team with a scientific approach to problem-solving and improvement design and evaluation. Through this collaborative improvement process, the team learned several lessons:

1. The problems associated with discharge planning, though complex, were interrelated. It was clear that the demands of managed care, expectations of patients and staff regarding hospitalization and discharge, multiple handoffs of patient information among clinicians across the continuum of care, and inefficient, sluggish hospital systems only compound the problem.

However, by systematically integrating patient feedback with process information, the discharge planning improvement team at Brigham and Women's Hospital established a solid foundation for subsequent improvement activity.

2. Feedback obtained through the PSS provided valuable, general information for monitoring processes and performance over time. However, carefully designed, patient-focused improvement activity requires a mechanism by which to elicit specific information directly from patients in a timely manner. Methods to ensure accurate interpretation of survey data, such as patient focus groups or interviews, are essential to continuous improvement efforts.

3. The hospital's automated clinical information systems provided essential support to the team in ensuring that patient handoffs from the hospital to the community

occurred seamlessly. By designing specific enhancements to the automated physicians' discharge summary program, follow-up information about each patient was down loaded to individual practices that contacted patients to schedule posthospital appointments. Such information system capabilities provide valuable assistance to future clinical innovations.

Reference

1. Hickey ML, Kleefield SF, Pearson SD, Hassan SM, Harding M, Haughie P, Lee TH, Brennan TA. Payer-hospital collaboration to improve patient satisfaction with hospital discharge. *Jt Comm J Qual Improv* 1996 May; 22(5):336-44.

The larger scope of patient satisfaction

The best practices listed throughout this book should be considered heavily condensed research, distilled for your understanding and guidance. However, simply dictating these best practices as marching orders for staff will have little efficacy, as our qualitative research never found command-and-control management practices employed among units with significant and sustained patient satisfaction improvement.

Instead, the way to introduce best practices to your facility is to deeply involve your staff. Make sure they have a part in developing solutions to the issues faced by your facility. An empowered staff will work harder toward a goal they feel is their goal too.

The following are nine overall best practices that your facility can use to run a tighter ship and ensure higher scores on patient satisfaction surveys. These best practices are drawn from the practices of the facilities that scored highest on the Press Ganey survey.

1. Strong, competent leadership of case management and patient education

Case management and patient education department leaders must be highly competent and effective. It will be difficult to improve performance in these areas with lackluster department leadership. Successful leadership intuitively understands the importance of patient satisfaction and manages staff using this and other metrics. Strong leaders will actively support the case managers and patient educators, serving their needs. Leaders will be invested in serving patients, frequently rounding and often handling cases themselves. The level of involvement by leadership is paramount to its understanding of what practices are and are not working.

2. Accountability for case managers

Hold case managers accountable for their performance, and measure that performance according to the following:

- ✔ Patient satisfaction with the discharge section
- ✔ Readmission rates
- ✔ Length of stay
- ✔ Percentage of patients receiving discharge planning services
- ✔ Percentage of patients with utilization review
- ✔ Peer review (using 360-degree feedback, chart review/evaluation, or some other tool)

3. Diverse use of tools and quality improvement methods

No single tool or quality improvement method was used more than any other in the hospitals that work with Press Ganey. Hospitals tended to use whatever tools they considered appropriate for the situation being analyzed or the intervention being implemented. Control charts, workflow diagrams, trending, process mapping, decision-trees, and causal analyses were all used in improvement initiatives.

4. Diverse organizational structures

Press Ganey has observed no pattern concerning the organizational structures for delivering patient care related to the discharge process. Successful hospitals of all sizes used various designs—from having an all-inclusive patient care management department that housed social workers, discharge planners, case managers, and utilization professionals, to having a separate department for each of these roles. Hospitals structured delivery of services related to discharge in various ways and had different professionals (social workers, management professionals, or nurses) fulfill these roles (e.g., discharge planning, patient education, coordination of posthospital services).

5. Advanced discharge services personnel beyond unit nurses

Despite diversity in structure, personnel, and organization of discharge-related care, high-performing hospitals consistently exhibited exceptional competence and organizational support for

Patient Satisfaction and the Discharge Process

advanced discharge services personnel. Although the charge nurses or the nurses providing care for that shift were involved in discharge, they were not the principal coordinators of discharge planning, education, or postdischarge services. Hospitals with exceptional patient satisfaction in the discharge process emphasized, supported, and expanded the discharge-related roles beyond unit nurses. Whether labeled *patient education, case management, or discharge planning,* hospitals strived toward 100% involvement in patient care for that role.

Making it work

Efforts at Claxton-Hepburn Medical Center (CHMC) in Ogdensburg, NY, to improve patient satisfaction included making changes to processes. CHMC identified a need to improve discharge planning from the question regarding help arranging home care services. In the past, case managers focused their attention only on patients who met criteria for home care services. Based on patient feedback, however, CMHC expanded assistance in planning for discharge to all patients. Each patient receives a letter of introduction and visit from a care manager. A list of questions encourages patients and family to discuss concerns such as living environment, transportation, nutrition, prescriptions, and payment for services.

6. Leadership support or prioritization

High-performing and most-improved hospitals initiated organizational changes as a result of prioritization of senior leadership. Several hospital executives simply placed high importance on patient education, patient flow, and customer service, and therefore dedicated considerable resources to expand these functions. For other hospitals, motivation for expanding the discharge services role and prioritization by senior leadership was a consequence of external pressures, such as changes in the sociodemographic makeup of the community increasing the demand for transitional care across the continuum of hospital to home. Appearance of discharge questions in the patient satisfaction priority index was not a sufficient motivator. Superlative leadership support and championship of discharge-related services and patient satisfaction were universal themes.

7. Customer service/behavioral standards

Every most-improved and highest-performing facility identified in our qualitative research based its success on a set of well-implemented customer service/behavioral standards. Staff typically draft the standards in a collaborative manner. All staff are held accountable for living the standards. The standards mirror the hospital's values, are integrated into the performance evaluations, and are a condition of employment. Everyone must sign an agreement to follow the standards.

Some organizations had standards but experienced a rejuvenation of their meaning, use, and importance through accountability.

Accountability meant enforcing the standards in evaluations and letting people go who would not agree to the standards or failed to meet these expectations. It also meant not hiring people who did not match the values of the organization or who did not agree to the standards.

Under the typical improvement pattern, customer service/behavioral standards diffused throughout the hospital and moderately improved patient satisfaction but then served as a launching pad to greater improvement trajectories. Widespread adoption of these standards was followed by the other practices detailed throughout this book, which collaboratively led to significant increases in patient satisfaction.

In hospitals today, customer service/behavioral standards are almost the status quo. If you do not have such standards, creating them is a first step. If you do have standards, review them. Ask yourself the following questions:

- Are they being followed?

- Do staff accept them?

- Do staff believe in the basic values of the hospital?

- Are staff evaluated on the basis of their adherence to the values and standards of the organization?

- Do managers believe in and follow the standards?

- Is management held accountable for these standards?

Some hospitals discover that they need to revise their standards or start anew if existing standards have become meaningless (e.g., standards no longer match the desired values and culture of the organization).

8. Read all patient comments; take rapid action
Most-improved and highest-scoring facilities all had a system for reading patients' comments and taking action to resolve problems raised. Typically, this system involved the nursing director, patient relations/customer service/service excellence position(s), and key department management/leadership. For example, one system gathers everyone in a weekly meeting to review surveys. Each patient comment is read aloud. Resolutions to problems are quickly identified, and responsibility for seeing the change or improvement through is volunteered or assigned. This meeting is held in a rapid-fire fashion and typically takes approximately one hour. Updates from the previous week's meeting are presented to ensure that past actions were executed.

 Patient Satisfaction and the Discharge Process

9. No silver bullet: Relentless execution of multiple proven practices

Patients want to go home. You want to get them home. Everyone wants throughput to work and work quickly, but there is no magic bullet. No one best practice is going to solve your facility's discharge-related shortcomings. Achieving significant and sustained success demands the relentless execution of multiple proven practices. The execution must be of high quality. But simply rolling out the initiative is not enough—it has to be used actively in daily practice. The lesson learned from interviewing multiple top performers and those that improved significantly is that patient satisfaction with the discharge process, as well as the

actual speed of discharge and patient flow, is within their control—they simply had to dive deep and not rely on one easy, obvious solution.

Conclusion

Patient satisfaction is within the reach of every facility. It won't happen overnight, and it won't happen as a result of one quick fix, but with dedication and a little hard work, it will happen. Stay true to your commitment to healthcare. You have the power to make a stressful, frustrating, and even frightening situation just a little more relaxing for the people who matter most: your patients.

Understanding your discharge process

A.1 FIGURE

Sample portion of a discharge process map

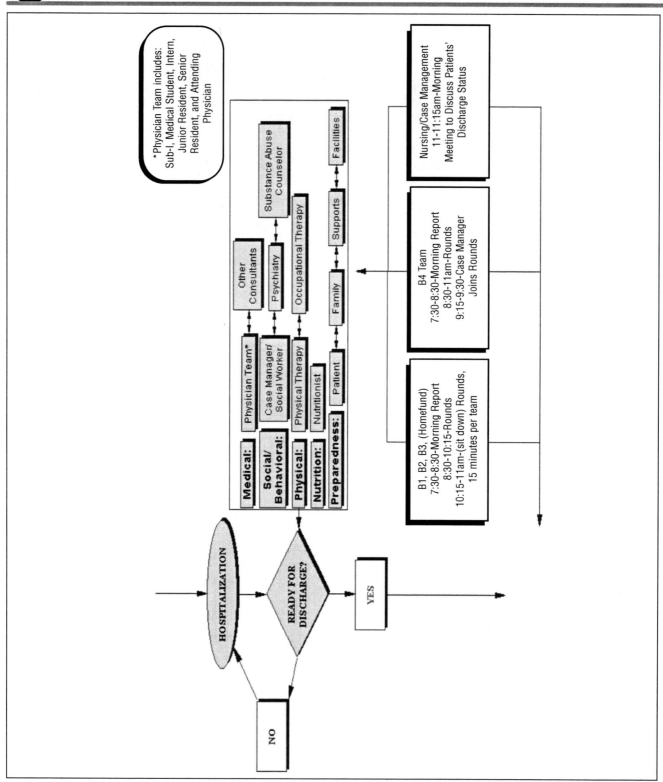

 Patient Satisfaction and the Discharge Process

Summary of JCAHO standards for patient education and AMA standards for discharge

A.1 TABLE

Joint Commission Standards

No.	Standard
PF.1	An assessment of the patient's learning needs, abilities, preferences, and readiness which considers culture, religion, emotional barriers, desire, motivation, physical and cognitive limitations, language barriers and financial implications (for the patient) and includes: • medication use education; medical equipment use education; information on drug-food interaction and counseling on nutrition; techniques to help patients adapt and function independently; information on community resources; • information on when and how to obtain any further treatment potentially needed; • elucidate to patients and families responsibilities for ongoing health care needs and the knowledge and skills to carry them out; • education and help maintaining good hygiene.
PF.2	Patient education is interactive.
PF.3	Provide discharge instructions to the responsible caregiver in addition to the patient or family.
PF.4	The hospital plans, supports, and coordinates activities and resources for patient and family education—including provision of all resources required and that this education process be collaborative and interdisciplinary.

American Medical Association Standards

No.	Standard
1.	**Discharge criteria** should be based on data from assessments of physiological, psychological, social and functional needs.
2.	**An interdisciplinary** team is necessary for comprehensive planning to meet the patient's needs.
3.	**Early assessment** and planning should be organized so that necessary personnel, equipment or training can be arranged in time for discharge.
4.	**Post-discharge medical care** requires arrangements (before discharge) for easy access to continuing physician care.
5.	**Patient and caregiver education** in meeting post-discharge patient needs should occur prior to discharge. Patients and caregivers should be able to demonstrate their understanding and ability to meet the care needs before discharge.
6.	Coordinated, timely and effective communication between all health professionals, caregivers and the patient is essential and should be well established before discharge.

Appendix A

Focused improvement worksheet

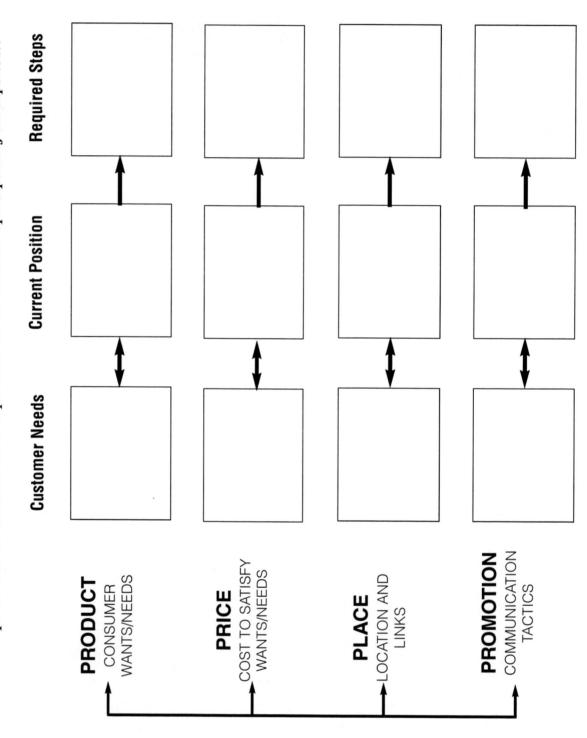

© 2006 Copyright HCPro, Inc. and Press Ganey Associates, Inc.   Patient Satisfaction and the Discharge Process

Levels of evidence for best practices

Evidence-based literature review and qualitative research methods

Patient satisfaction is one outcome of a healthcare organization's structures and processes;[1] it is an indicator of both quality of care and quality of healthcare service. To determine best practices for improving patient satisfaction, Press Ganey applies well-recognized, scientifically sound methods for evaluating evidence.[2] This approach, initially applied to medical decision-making to ensure scientifically sound treatment decisions,[3] has recently been extended to determine best practices for improving other quality outcomes.[4]

For each analysis, we conduct multiple structure literature searches across a variety of databases (e.g., PubMed/Medline, CINAHL, Ovid, etc.). The resulting studies are critically evaluated to determine the strength or level of evidence (see Table B.1), and relevant findings are extracted and synthesized to compose a systematic literature review. Independently, we conduct a series of qualitative interviews with staff at hospitals that exhibit high performance or the most significant improvement in the area under investigation. Persons most directly involved in that area are included in the interview (e.g., quality improvement professionals, nurses, nursing unit managers, department heads, doctors, etc.). Best-performing and most-improved facilities are determined by using an algorithm that eliminates potential spuriousness such as random variation. In this way, best practices are supported by both quantitative and qualitative research.

B.1 TABLE   Levels of evidence

• **Level I:** Systematic literature review of randomized controlled trials (RCT). The practice has proven by multiple RCTs to improve patient satisfaction. Review searches for the existence of any evidence to the contrary and factors such evidence into consideration.

• **Level II:** RCTs in which at least one study has shown a cause and effect. Limitations usually apply, as RCTs frequently draw on limited populations.

• **Level III:** Pseudo-randomized, comparative studies with control and comparative studies with historical control. Limitations always apply to the generalizability of these studies.

• **Level IV:** Case series or case study. Usually uncontrolled; therefore, cause and effect cannot be assumed. Practice used, possibly as part of a cadre of interventions. Holds only the potential for efficacy. Serious limitations on generalizability.

• **Level V:** Unpublished studies of interventions to improve patient satisfaction. Usually not controlled. Almost always one component of several interventions or an overarching organizational change. Cause and effect cannot be determined.

When resources and finances are limited, it's important to focus on improvements that will best benefit your facility. These levels will help you to make a more informed decision about which practices your facility might choose to pursue.

While we recognize that healthcare organizations have an immediate imperative to improve patient satisfaction, we suggest that you consider all the improvements, even those that show low evidence levels. The analysis serves to indicate the efficacy and strength of evidence behind each practice. When implementing a practice with a low evidence level, adjust your expectations and recognize that generalizability is limited. The analysis allows for a prioritization of interventions given that higher evidence levels tend to carry a greater likelihood of effective improvement. Finally, the

evidence levels are not absolute predictors of success, simply current indicators of generalizability. A practice may be at Level V simply because it is too recent an innovation to be fully researched and published.

These methods result in a synthesis of existing, published knowledge with the additional advantage of original qualitative research that offers previously uncodified, tacit knowledge. This combination forms the cadre of evidence-based best practices proven to improve patient satisfaction that are now at your fingertips.

      Patient Satisfaction and the Discharge Process

Survey research methods

Every year Press Ganey surveys millions of
patients and thousands of nurses and physicians
in partnership with thousands of healthcare
organizations in order to help them improve
their customer experiences. Data represent 33%
of all U.S. hospitals and 44% of all U.S. hospitals with more than 100 beds. A research firm
specializing in satisfaction measurement within
the healthcare industry, we collect and house
data for hospitals across the United States for
the purposes of quality improvement and bench-
marking.

All our survey methodologies adhere to established good practice.[5] Questionnaires are mailed
immediately following a patient's discharge from
an acute-care facility. Patients received the surveys well within the six-week time frame recommended by Brédart et al. (2002) and typically
within 15 days from discharge.[6] The sample was
drawn from more than 1,500 acute-care facilities
across all 50 states and the District of Columbia.
Each facility sampled patients using standard
random sampling procedures or conducted cen-
sus. Repeat patients within one quarter, deaths,
and newborns were excluded from the samples.
Facilities survey either all discharged patients or
a random sample of patients. The methods
detailed here have been applied to assess service
quality and patient satisfaction on national and
local levels across a variety of settings.

The standard patient satisfaction survey includes
49 questions separated into 10 sections that
cover the complete hospitalization experience
from admission to discharge. It employs a five-
point Likert-type response scale: (1) very poor,
(2) poor, (3) fair, (4) good, (5) very good. Cover
letters accompany the survey. Their exact word-
ing varies by hospital, but all cover letters are
subject to two explicit standards to ensure data
quality: (a) no persuading comments (e.g.,
"Thank you for helping us . . . as we strive for
5s") and (b) no inclusion of the phrase "very
good" or reference to "5" or "five."

The overall patient satisfaction score implicitly
indexes global satisfaction and is calculated by
averaging the ratings for all individual survey
items by each section to determine a section
mean score. Then all section mean scores are
averaged to determine the overall patient satisfaction score. To improve data interpretation
and analysis of score variation, the 1–5 scale is
converted using a linear transformation to a
0–100 score where very poor = 0, poor = 25,
fair = 50, good = 75, and very good = 100. This
degree of measurement is sensitive enough to
detect small changes in patient satisfaction. This
is important because small changes can result in
large movements in national and state rankings.

Survey theory and development
The order of survey sections was determined by
a typical inpatient visit. It is designed to mimic
the patient experience, allowing for easier

patient recall and more accurate evaluations. To wit:

When patients first arrive, they must be admitted (Admission) and taken to a room (Room). If they are there for any length of time, they will next encounter personnel and be served one or more meals (Meals, Nurses). Typically, sometime they will encounter tests and treatments (Tests and Treatments). They may have family present (Visitors and Family). The physician will check in on them during rounds (Physician). They are discharged (Discharge).

These are the "discrete" episodes of hospitalization. There are other, more global experiences that are important to the total perception of care, as well. First, throughout the patient's stay, hospital personnel are either attentive or not attentive to the patient's personal needs, preferences, concerns, and worries. These are examined under "Personal Issues." Second, once the patient has been asked to review all of the hospital experiences, he or she is in a good position to make overall ratings. Thus, the "Overall" section of the survey follows the rest of the section.

Press Ganey surveys allow patients the chance to evaluate processes before they are asked to evaluate the primary staff involved in their care, leading to a more stringent assessment of the experience. Patients have a harder time providing criticism regarding other people, especially those who have more perceived power than they do. By putting the process issues first, you allow patients

to become more comfortable with evaluating the experience so that they can provide honest answers throughout the survey.

Psychometrics

The survey is rigorously tested and exceeds all psychometric standards for reliability and validity. These analyses validate the grouping of each question in a given section and the sections, including discharge, into the overall satisfaction with experience of care survey.

Reliability

The internal consistency/reliability of the survey was determined by calculating Cronbach's alpha statistic for each scale and for the entire instrument. Cronbach's alpha measures reliability across repeated tests using a scale of value between 0 and 1, with 1 indicating higher reliability. Alphas for the scales range from 0.84 to 0.95, and Cronbach's alpha for the entire instrument was 0.98, confirming its high internal consistency/reliability.

Validity

Construct validity assesses whether the conceptual model that forms the basis of the survey reflects distinctions made by patients as they fill out the scale. Do patients rate items within a subscale in a coherent way? Construct validity was determined by factor analysis, which yielded nine factors mirroring the subsections of the questionnaire. An item should be correlated with its own scale (convergent validity) as well as correlated more with its own scale than with other scales

 Patient Satisfaction and the Discharge Process

(discriminant validity). Convergent validity is demonstrated by the average correlations between each item and its parent scale, corrected for the contribution made by the particular item in question. Average corrected item-scale correlations for the subsections of the Inpatient Survey range from 0.62 to 0.86. Discriminant validity is shown by the fact that, on average, items from each scale correlate with items from other scales from 0.40 to 0.59. Predictive validity, the ability of an instrument to predict outcomes that theoretically should be tied to the construct measured by the instrument, is measured by the relationship of individual items (and the entire scale) to the patient's reported likelihood of recommending the facility to others, a measure of "positive word of mouth." Multiple regression analysis revealed that, collectively, all items are significant predictors of patients' reported likelihood to recommend the hospital, explaining approximately 77% of the variance in that measure.

More information about the psychometric properties of the Press Ganey Inpatient Survey can be obtained from the author, or found in Kaldenberg, Mylod & Drain (2001).[7]

References

1. A. Donabedian, *Exploration in Quality Assessment and Monitoring: The Definition of Quality and Approaches to Its Assessment.* Vol 1. Ann Arbor, MI: Health Administration Press, 1980; A. Donabedian, "Quality, Cost, and Clinical Decisions," *Annals of the American Academy of Political and Social Science* 468 (1983): 196–204; A. Donabedian, "Quality Assessment and Assurance: Unity of Purpose, Diversity of Means," *Inquiry* 25, no. 1 (1988): 173–192.

2. U.S. Preventive Services Task Force, *Guide to Clinical Preventive Services.* Baltimore, MD: U.S. Preventive Services Task Force, 1996; University of California at San Francisco-Stanford University Evidence-based Practice Center, "Evidence-Based Review Methodology," in *Making Health Care Safer: A Critical Analysis of Patient Safety Practices*, edited by K. G. Shojania and others. Washington, DC: AHRQ, 2003; G. H. Guyatt and others, "Users' Guides to the Medical Literature: XVI. How to Use a Treatment Recommendation. Evidence-Based Medicine Working Group and the Cochrane Applicability Methods Working Group," *Journal of the American Medical Association* 281, no. 19 (1999): 1836–1843.

3. J. T. Hart, "What Evidence Do We Need for Evidence Based Medicine?" *Journal of Epidemiology and Community Health* 51, no. 6 (1997): 623–629; D. L. Olive and E. A. Pritts, "What is Evidence-Based Medicine?" *Journal of the American Association of Gynecologic Laparoscopists* 4, no. 5 (1997): 615–621; J. Arya, H. Wolford, and A. H. Harken, "Evidence-Based Science: A Worthwhile Mode of Surgical Inquiry," *Archives of Surgery* 137, no. 11 (2002):

1301–1303; S. Buetow and T. Kenealy, "Evidence-Based Medicine: The Need for a New Definition," *Journal of Evaluation in Clinical Practice* 6, no. 2 (2000): 85–92; F. Davidoff, "In the Teeth of the Evidence: The Curious Case of Evidence-Based Medicine," *Mount Sinai Journal of Medicine* 66, no. 2 (1999): 75–83; R. R. West, "Evidence Based Medicine Overviews, Bulletins, Guidelines, and the New Consensus," *Journal of Postgraduate Medicine* 76, no. 897 (2000): 383–389.

4. K. G. Shojania and others, "Safe But Sound: Patient Safety Meets Evidence-Based Medicine," *Journal of the American Medical Association* 288, no. 4 (2002): 508–513; L. L. Leape, D. M. Berwick, and D. W. Bates, "What Practices Will Most Improve Safety? Evidence-Based Medicine Meets Patient Safety," *Journal of the American*

Medical Association 288, no. 4 (2002): 501–507.

5. K. Kelley and others, "Good Practice in the Conduct and Reporting of Survey Research," *International Journal for Quality in Health Care* 15 (2003): 261–266.

6. A. Bredart and others, "Timing of Patient Satisfaction Assessment: Effect on Questionnaire Acceptability, Completeness of Data, Reliability and Variability of Scores," *Patient Education and Counseling* 46 (2002): 131–136.

7. D. O. Kaldenberg, D. E. Mylod, and M. Drain, "Patient-Derived Information: Satisfaction with Care in Acute and Post-Acute Care Environments," *in Measuring and Managing Health Care Quality*, ed. N. Goldfield, M. Pine, and J. Pine (Rockville, MD: Aspen Publishers, 2003), 4:69–4:89.

Sample thank you card language

SHARP. Chula Vista Medical Center

Thank you for allowing us at Sharp Chula Vista to take care of you.

In a few weeks, you may receive a survey in the mail from us. Please take a moment to complete and return it.

Our surveys use a 5-point scale, with 5 as the highest rating. If we deserve less than a 5, please let us know how we can improve.

We care very much about your comments because they help us improve our service to others. They also help us train, reward and recognize our staff.

Thank you again for the privilege of serving you.

    Patient Satisfaction and the Discharge Process

Sample family caregiver assessments

© 2006 Copyright HCPro, Inc. and Press Ganey Associates, Inc.

A. The family caregiver needs assessment

Role needs:

- What does the caregiver know about the elder's disease or illness?
- Can the caregiver distinguish symptoms related to normal aging from complications related to illness?
- Does the caregiver know signs of adverse reactions to medications?
- Does the caregiver have questions about special diets or treatment plans?
- What are the caregiver's expectations about the illness trajectory?
- Does the caregiver feel confident about his or her skills and time management?
- What tasks would the caregiver like help with?
- Any financial concerns related to caregiving or health insurance coverage?

Caregiver's health

- How is the caregiver coping?
- Any concerns about own health?
- To whom does he or she turn when he or she needs help?
- To what extent is the help he or she receives meeting his or her needs?
- Does the family caregiver feel abandoned by other family members?

From: J.M. Bull and R. E. McShane, "Needs and Supports for Family Caregivers of Elders," *Journal of Home Healthcare Management and Practice* 14, no. 2 (2002): 88–94.

B. The family preparedness assessment

1. In what way is the family at risk?

- How was the family system functioning before the illness, and how has the illness altered the balance?
- In what ways are the patient and family able to help one another's burdens?
- Does the family have access to whatever resources they need to cope effectively?
- What are the epidemiologic risks, and how are these perceived by the family?
- Is anyone concerned about infectious or genetic or indirect effects on other family members, and does the family need counseling or further discussion in this regard?

2. What is the family's role in this patient's care and treatment?

- What are their strengths?
- What are the family's views of illness in general?
- Do they regard the illness as a stigma or punishment for previous sins or as a ticket to avoiding responsibility?
- Are their views consonant with those of the patient, yourself, and other medical personnel involved?
- What are the family's views on medical care?
- Do they view you and/or hospitals positively or negatively?

- Will you be working together on the patient's treatment or at cross purposes?

3. During hospitalization, is the family able to spend quality time with the patient?
   - Do they have reasonably private moments together, free of staff and activity?
   - What can be done to help them find some moments together?

4. How do hospital staff and you view the family?
   - Do they (you) think of the family in respectful terms?

- Are they (you) beginning to think of the family as nuisances, idiots, turkeys, or adversaries?
- How much are staff attitudes contributing to interactional problems?
- In what ways can attitudes be altered to facilitate more empathetic and effective treatment?

From: M. R. Lipp, *Respectful Treatment: The Human Side of Medical Care.* (New York: Elsevier), 1986: 172–178.

Sample phone
tips and scripts

Who makes the phone calls?

Most facilities want nurses to make the calls so that they can immediately address any health/clinical issues that patients may bring up. These nurses are typically

- in the recovery area and have down time at the beginning of the day

- those who assist in procedures and have down time at the end of the day

- older nurses looking for part-time and/or less physically demanding work

Many other facilities have no problem utilizing nonclinical staff members, including

- front desk and reception personnel who will have down time at various times throughout the day

- secretaries and patient care assistants on the unit

- call center personnel

For those facilities that use nonclinical staff, clinical questions result either in paging clinical staff or going to their voice mail. Arm your nonclinical staff with triage questions that they can use to determine whether the issue is of an emergent nature and the caller needs to go to the ED.

Some facilities utilize physicians to make phone calls. This is most typical among outpatient or ambulatory surgery procedures. Patients may not have seen their physician before returning home. Rekindling that relationship has benefits in patient satisfaction and loyalty with both the healthcare organization and the physician. The fact is, patients, particularly after outpatient and ambulatory surgery care, want to talk with their physician. They will often call physicians after their discharge. By having physicians call them first, it preempts these calls and boosts patient satisfaction.

Post-procedure phone calls

- Within 24–48 hours of encounter.
- Review discharge instructions.
- Solicit opinion: ask patients what they thought about the process.

  - When you start, be prepared to record a lot of feedback, especially if you are not far along in your patient satisfaction journey. You will discover a great deal of direct, actionable feedback.
  - As you address this feedback as well as specific comments on your patient satisfaction surveys, the volume of negative feedback you receive will decline.
  - Feed the comments back to supervisors and appropriate quality management professionals to achieve full service recovery potential.

 Patient Satisfaction and the Discharge Process

- Record comments, patient name, and other information.

- Remind patients about survey coming in the mail.

- Reward individuals:
  - Promote, post, and reward staff members identified by former patients with positive comments.

- Add this data to your complaint management database.

Leaving messages for patients during pre- and post-procedure phone calls

Pre- and post-procedure, many facilities conduct phone calls to evaluate patient needs. It gives patients an opportunity to ask questions and provide feedback. Unfortunately with today's fast-paced lifestyle, actually reaching patients at their residence can be problematic. However, leaving messages for patients becomes a problem because of the Health Insurance Portability and Accountability Act of 1996 (HIPAA) regulations regarding patient privacy. See *www.hipaadvisory.com/action/privacy/daytoday.htm* for more information about HIPAA.

We recommend that messages are not left for pre- and post-op calls. Due to the importance of the information exchange and the potential HIPAA

violations, hospitals may see little benefit to leaving messages.

When the patient is not at home but a caller is reached, use a script, such as the following:

Nurse: Good day, is Ms. Jones there?
Receiver: No, I'm sorry she is not.
Nurse: Do you know of a good time for me to reach her?
Receiver: I'm not sure. I can have her call you back.
Nurse: I appreciate that, but it may be simpler for me to reach her.
Receiver: May I tell her what this is in regard to?
Nurse: No, thank you. Thank you for your assistance and have a great day.

If the hospital chooses to adopt a policy for leaving messages, it must meet the following criteria:

- A statement must be made in the facility's Notice of Privacy Practices regarding pre- and post-op phone calls.

- Patients must have a way to opt out of the phone calls/messages, and this needs to be accounted for in the call-system. A mark on the chart that the nurse completing the phone call will never see is unacceptable.

- The message should include as little information as possible. Do not mention the physician specialty, procedure, admission dates, etc., as this is all privileged information.

Sample message

Good morning, I'm calling for Ms. Smith. This is Jeanie from your doctor's office. If you could, please give me a call back at 555-2424 and ask for Jeanie or another available nurse anytime between 8–5 Monday through Friday. It would be greatly appreciated. Thank you and have a wonderful day.

Make sure patients who do call back can be quickly serviced. Keeping patient charts who are not reachable in a specific location and having a nurse available to speak to those patients are essentials to an effective system. Do not provide only a general hospital or office number that will require several transfers before patients can speak to the correct person. The process needs to be simple and accessible for patients to make leaving messages an effective tool.

     Patient Satisfaction and the Discharge Process

Nursing and physician continuing education instruction guide

Target Audience:

- Directors and Managers of Quality
- Patient Satisfaction Directors and Patient Representatives
- Risk Managers
- Directors of Nursing , Staff nurses, Nurse Managers
- Directors of Case Management , Case Managers
- Social Workers and Discharge Planners
- Physician executives, Hospitalists

Statement of Need:

This hands-on, how-to guide contains best practices pulled from data gathered from tens of thousands of patient survey responses in more than 6,000 facilities nationwide. *Patient Satisfaction and the Discharge Process* offers a collection of strategies for providing a successful discharge experience for readers' patients. The book will help healthcare administrators and professionals make measurable improvements to their facility discharge planning process.

Patient Satisfaction and the Discharge Process brings together the key national studies and the standards of leading agencies—including CMS, the JCAHO, and the AMA—on discharge process. It offers the applicable data, relevant research, and proven strategies to aid in quickly and effectively implementing a high quality discharge planning program under HCAHPS—CMS' new initiative to publicly report patient perceptions of care.

Educational Objectives:

Upon completion of this activity, participants should be able to

- define the differences between patient causes and hospital causes of dissatisfaction with the discharge process
- describe the key elements of the AMA Guidance on the components of a quality discharge process
- list three things hospitals may do that make patients feel rushed
- describe two things hospitals do to cause low scores on patient satisfaction with the speed of discharge
- identify three questions staff can ask patients that may elicit unspoken concerns or needs
- describe five basic living activities that the patient will face post-discharge and that may lead them to not feel confident that they can care for themselves
- discuss why it is important to have variation in educational resources
- create an outline for an effective family caregiver assessment
- describe the potential impact of post-discharge callbacks and home visits on patient concerns about unanticipated needs arising post-discharge
- describe the role and use of "education nurses" at one hospital to successfully improve follow-up and patient satisfaction

Faculty

Paul Alexander Clark, MPA, MA, CHE, is the Senior Knowledge Manager for Press Ganey Associates. He directs a team of researchers who conduct quantitative and qualitative research to determine best practices for improving patient, employee, and physician satisfaction in healthcare. His team's research supports more than 110 Press Ganey consultants who actively partner with healthcare organizations to help improve the service they provide to patients, employees, and physi-

 Patient Satisfaction and the Discharge Process

cians. Clark earned a Master of Public Administration in Science and Technology Policy from George Mason University in Fairfax, VA, a Master of Arts in Bioethics and Healthcare Policy at the Loyola University in Chicago, and a bachelor's degree from the University of Pittsburgh. He is currently a member of the University of North Carolina's Executive MHA program and a Diplomate in the American College of Healthcare Executives.

Accreditation Statements:

Nursing:
HCPro is accredited as a provider of continuing nursing education by the American Nurses Credentialing Center Commission on Accreditation.

CME:
HCPro, Inc. is accredited by the Accreditation Council for Continuing Medical Education to provide continuing medical education for physicians.

Credit Designation Statements:

Nursing:
This educational activity for 3 nursing contact hours is provided by HCPro, Inc.

CME:
HCPro, Inc. designates this educational activity for a maximum of 3 AMA PRA Category 1 Credit(s)™. Physicians should only claim credit commensurate with the extent of their participation in the activity.

Disclosure Statements

HCPro, Inc. has a conflict of interest policy that requires course faculty to disclose any real or apparent commercial financial affiliations related to the content of their presentations/materials. It is not assumed that these financial interests or affiliations will have an adverse impact on faculty presentations; they are simply noted here to fully inform the participants.

Instructions

In order to be eligible to receive your nursing contact hours or physician continuing education credits for this activity, you are required to do the following:

1. Read the book, *Patient Satisfaction and the Discharge Planning Process: Evidence-Based Best Practices*
2. Complete the exam
3. Complete the evaluation
4. Provide your contact information on the exam and evaluation
5. Submit exam and evaluation to HCPro, Inc.

Please provide all of the information requested above and mail or fax your completed exam, program evaluation, and contact information to

Robin L. Flynn
Manager, Continuing Education
HCPro, Inc.
200 Hoods Lane
P.O. Box 1168
Marblehead, MA 01945
Fax: 781/639-0179

NOTE:

This book and associated exam are intended for individual use only. If you would like to provide this continuing education exam to other members of your nursing or physician staff, please contact our customer service department at 877/727-1728 to place your order. The exam fee schedule is as follows:

Exam Quantity Fee

1	$0	51 – 100	$8 per person
2 – 25	$15 per person	101+	$5 per person
26 – 50	$12 per person		

Continuing Education Exam

Name: _____

Title: _____

Facility Name: _____

Address: _____

Address: _____

City: _____ State: _____ Zip: _____

Phone Number: _____ Fax Number: _____

E-mail: _____

Date Completed: _____

1. Which of the following is a <u>patient</u> cause for dissatisfaction with the discharge process?

    a. A bed shortage

    b. Expectations of a short hospital stay and quick recovery

    c. Ineffective education materials

    d. Failure to develop a long-term relationship between hospital and patient

2. Why is it a <u>hospital</u> cause of dissatisfaction when arrangements for activities of daily living are not made?

    a. Patients should be aware of their own limitations.

    b. Hospitals should presume that **all** patients need home health assistance.

    c. Hospital staff should be aware of and sensitive to individual patient physical limiations.

    d. It isn't. Education materials should arm the patient with enough resources for such help.

3. Which of the following is <u>not</u> part of the American Medical Association's guidance for quality discharge?

  a. Get well incentives, such as meal vouchers

  b. Postdischarge medical care

  c. Patient and caregiver education

  d. An interdisciplinary team to meet patient needs

4. According to the AMA, discharge criteria should be based on data from what kind of assessment?

  a. Functional

  b. Physiological

  c. Social

  d. All of the above

5. What is one way to reassure a patient that he is not being rushed?

  a. Tell the patient he looks strong and should consider packing his belongings because other people need the bed more.

  b. Send the patient to a step-down unit where he can consider his options for postdischarge.

  c. Keep telling the patient he's fine and progressing well, even if it's untrue.

  d. Keep the physician away from the patient so the physician doesn't "bring the patient down."

6. If your organization experiences low scores on the survey question regarding speed of discharge, consider

  a. cutting that last patient-physician visit to save time

  b. keeping discharge times vague so the patient won't have high expectations

  c. daily rounding so case managers know the status of each patient and can answer patient questions

  d. keeping only the surveys that look favorably on your organization

    Patient Satisfaction and the Discharge Process

7. What can a transition coordinator do to ensure that the day of discharge goes smoothly?

    a. Review the day's schedule with the patient

    b. Obtain additional educational materials for the patient and family

    c. See that the patient has considered transportation needs for leaving the hospital

    d. All of the above

8. Which of the following is <u>not</u> an appropriate question that may elicit unspoken concerns?

    a. Are you in pain?

    b. Is there anything you are worried about?

    c. Have your children come to visit you?

    d. Can you show me how you will do your exercises?

9. What is one thing you can say to calm a patient before a stressful test?

    a. You're not nervous, are you?

    b. Will you try a breathing exercise with me?

    c. You're smart and strong; I'm sure you'll ace this.

    d. It's just a quick needle—nothing to be afraid of.

10. Which of the following is an easy, effective way for patients, caregivers, and staff to maintain awareness of ADLs?

    a. A "ticket home" sign in the patient's room that lists physical milestones

    b. Word of mouth among staff

    c. Make the case manager solely responsible for that information

    d. Large boards posted at the nurse station that list patient names and physical limitations

11. Which of the following is an ADL that the patient may not have anticipated being a difficulty at the time of discharge?

    a. Grocery shopping

    b. Climbing stairs

    c. Driving

    d. All of the above

12. Written patient education materials should be

    a. technical so patients can better understand their status and perform research on their own

    b. kept at a 5th to 6th grade reading and comprehension level so they are easily understood

    c. kept at an 11th to 12th grade reading and comprehension level so patients don't feel they are being spoken down to

    d. only in English; patients need to know to speak up if anything is unclear

13. Why is it important to have variation among educational resources?

    a. It isn't. Focus on one medium and do it well.

    b. To make sure all patients, regardless of age or ability, receive the information they need.

    c. So the staff can choose their personal favorite to present to each patient.

    d. None of the above.

14. Which of the following is <u>not</u> a best practice followed by a top-scoring hospital?

    a. Having physicians make follow-up patient calls

    b. Weekly quality improvement meetings

    c. Working to narrow down the amount of information the patient receives

    d. Asking patients to simulate aspects of home care before discharge

     Patient Satisfaction and the Discharge Process

15. How can an organization benefit from the role of education nurses?

    a. Education nurses can pass along information on conditions in which they specialize to colleagues, saving them time

    b. Nurses can specialize in different conditions, and stay current on that information

    c. Patients will receive more thorough answers to their questions regarding illness

    d. All of the above

16. What does PDCA stand for?

    a. Preliminary, during, current, other

    b. Plan, do, check, act

    c. Plan, demonstrate, check, act

    d. Patient-doctor contract agreement

17. How did Harvard Community Health Plan challenge Brigham and Women's Hospital to increase patient satisfaction ratings?

    a. It offered to work more closely with the hospital

    b. It threatened to pull out of the relationship

    c. It offered a financial incentive

    d. It pitted the hospital against other area hospitals in a citywide challenge

18. Choose the action most likely to help improve patient satisfaction:

    a. Providing multimedia education resources

    b. Having an inexperienced volunteer call patients postdischarge

    c. Creating a communication buffer between patients and physicians

    d. Exaggerating the expected discharge date so the patient is discharged substantially earlier

19. Which of the following services can case managers provide if they round daily?

a. They can tell patients the status of any outstanding tests

b. They can provide an explanation of any home care services

c. They can confirm that all discharge plans meet the patient's wishes

d. All of the above

20. Why is patient education prior to admission important?

a. It helps to establish an understanding of any symptoms the patient may experience

b. The patient will enter the facility with a better understanding of what staff will do to help them

c. The patient will be able to better anticipate how much pain he or she may feel during recovery

d. All of the above

    Patient Satisfaction and the Discharge Process

Continuing Education Evaluation

Name: _____

Title: _____

Facility Name: _____

Address: _____

Address: _____

City: _____ State: _____ Zip: _____

Phone Number: _____ Fax Number: _____

E-mail: _____

1. **This activity met the learning objectives stated:**

    Strongly Agree   Agree   Disagree   Strongly Disagree

2. **Objectives were related to the overall purpose/goal of the activity:**

    Strongly Agree   Agree   Disagree   Strongly Disagree

3. **This activity was related to my continuing education needs:**

    Strongly Agree   Agree   Disagree   Strongly Disagree

4. **The exam for the activity was an accurate test of the knowledge gained:**

    Strongly Agree   Agree   Disagree   Strongly Disagree

5. **The activity avoided commercial bias or influence:**

    Strongly Agree   Agree   Disagree   Strongly Disagree

6. **This activity met my expectations:**

    Strongly Agree   Agree   Disagree   Strongly Disagree

7. Will this activity enhance your professional practice?

     Yes   No

8. The format was an appropriate method for delivery of the content for this activity:

     Strongly Agree   Agree   Disagree   Strongly Disagree

9. Please indicate whether you are requesting Nursing Contact Hours or Physician Continuing Education Credits (CME) with this publication.

10. If you have any comments on this activity please note them here:

11. How much time did it take for you to complete this activity?

Thank you for completing this evaluation of our continuing education activity!

Return completed form to:

HCPro, Inc. • Attn: Robin L. Flynn • 200 Hoods Lane, Marblehead, MA 01945 •Tel 877/727-1728 • Fax 781/639-2982

 Patient Satisfaction and the Discharge Process